FITZGERALD/HEMINGWAY ANNUAL 1969

Edited by Matthew J. Bruccoli
University of South Carolina

NCR **MICROCARD® EDITIONS**
901 TWENTY-SIXTH STREET, N.W., WASHINGTON, D. C. 20037, 202/333-6393
INDUSTRIAL PRODUCTS DIVISION, THE NATIONAL CASH REGISTER COMPANY

Editor: Matthew J. Bruccoli

Department of English
University of South Carolina
Columbia, S. C. 29208

Associate Editor: C. E. Frazer Clark, Jr.

1490 Sodon Lake Drive
Bloomfield Hills, Michigan 48013

Address all editorial correspondence to the editors.

Address orders and inquiries to Microcard Editions, 901 26th
Street, N.W., Washington, D.C. 20037.

Charles A. Fenton

1919 - 1960

Contents

Dearly Beloved

By

F. Scott Fitzgerald*

O my Beauty Boy—reading Plato so divine! O, dark, oh fair, colored golf champion of Chicago. Over the rails he goes at night, steward of the club car, and afterwards in the dim smoke by the one light and the smell of stale spittoons, writing west to the Rosecrucian Brotherhood. Seeking ever.

O Beauty Boy here is your girl, not one to soar like you, but a clean swift serpent who will travel as fast on land and look toward you in the sky.

Lilymary loved him, oft invited him and they were married in St. Jarvis' church in North Englewood. For years they bettered themselves, running along the tread-mill of their race, becoming only a little older and no better than before. He was loaned the Communist Manifesto by the wife of the advertising manager of a Chicago daily but for preference give him Plato—the Phaedo and the Apologia, or else the literature of the Rosecrucian Brotherhood of Sacramento, California, which burned in his ears as the rails clicked past Alton, Springfield and Burlington in the dark.

Bronze lovers, never never canst thou have thy bronze child— or so it seemed for years. Then the clock struck, the gong rang and Dr. Edwin Burch of South Michigan Avenue agreed to han-

1

dle the whole thing for two hundred dollars. They looked so nice—so delicately nice, neither of them ever hurting the other and gracefully expert in the avoidance. Beauty Boy took fine care of her in her pregnancy—paid his sister to watch with her while he did double work on the road and served for caterers in the city; and one day the bronze baby was born.

O Beauty Boy, Lilymary said, here is your beauty boy. She lay in a four bed ward in the hospital with the wives of a prize fighter, an undertaker and a doctor. Beauty Boy's face was so twisted with radiance; his teeth shining so in his smile and his eyes so kind that it seemed that nothing and nothing could ever.

Beauty Boy sat beside her bed when she slept and read Thoreau's Walden for the third time. Then the nurse told him he must leave. He went on the road that night and in Alton going to mail a letter for a passenger he slipped under the moving train and his leg was off above the knee.

Beauty Boy lay in the hospital and a year passed. Lilymary went back to work again cooking. Things were tough, there was even trouble about his workman's compensation, but he found lines in his books that helped them along for awhile when all the human beings seemed away.

The little baby flourished but he was not beautiful like his parents; not as they had expected in those golden dreams. They had only spare-time love to give the child so the sister more and more and more took care of him. For they wanted to get back where they were, they wanted Beauty Boy's leg to grow again so it would all be like it was before. So that he could find delight in his books again and Lilymary could find delight in hoping for a little baby.

Some years passed. They were so far back on the tread-mill that they would never catch up. Beauty Boy was a night-watchman now but he had six operations on his stump and each new artificial limb gave him constant pain. Lilymary worked fairly steadily as a cook. Now they had become just ordinary people. Even the sister had long since forgotten that Beauty

Boy was formerly colored golf champion of Chicago. Once in cleaning the closet she threw out all his books—the Apologia and the Phaedo of Plato, and the Thoreau and the Emerson and all the leaflets and correspondence with the Rosecrucian Brotherhood. He didn't find out for a long time that they were gone. And then he just stared at the place where they had been and said "Say, man . . . say man."

For things change and get so different that we can hardly recognize them and it seems that only our names remain the same. It seemed wrong for them still to call each other Beauty Boy and Lilymary long after the delight was over.

Some years later they both died in an influenza epidemic and went to heaven. They thought it was going to be all right then— indeed things began to happen in exactly the way that they had been told as children. Beauty Boy's leg grew again and he became golf champion of all heaven, both white and black, and drove the ball powerfully from cloud to cloud through the blue fairway. Lilymary's breasts became young and firm, she was respected among the other angels, and her pride in Beauty Boy became as it had been before.

In the evening they sat and tried to remember what it was they missed. It was not his books, for here everyone knew all those things by heart, and it was not the little boy for he had never really been one of them. They couldn't remember so after a puzzled time they would give up trying, and talk about how nice the other one was, or how fine a score Beauty Boy would make tomorrow.

So things go.

---

*This previously unpublished story is printed from a typescript in the Fitzgerald Papers, Princeton University Library. It is published here with the generous permission of Frances Scott Fitzgerald Smith.

Josephine And Emotional Bankruptcy

By

Constance Drake

In *The Far Side of Paradise*, Arthur Mizener states that Fitzgerald's theory of "emotional bankruptcy" was "the most pervasive idea he ever had . . . ."[1] Because its pervasiveness has been recognized by many critics, application of this theory has become a standard approach to Fitzgerald's most significant work. Mizener sees it as essential to understanding *Tender Is the Night* and *The Last Tycoon*; Richard Lehan applies it with varying degrees of directness and detail to *The Beautiful and the Damned* (as does Kenneth Eble) as well as *Tender Is the Night* and *The Last Tycoon*, and both Mizener and Lehan recognize the importance of *The Crack Up* as an autobiographical depiction of the concept.[2]

Yet "emotional bankruptcy" is generally regarded as a simple theory which can be explained merely as the loss of the ability to feel because one has wasted his emotions and has no more left to spend. Because there is little attempt to discover just what kind of person wastes them, or how or why he wastes them, the importance of the Josephine stories—the series in which Fitzgerald both applied and clarified his theory for the first time—is consistently overlooked or minimized. Both Lehan and Henry Dan Piper fail to recognize the relationship of the series to the theory altogether,[3] while Eble and Mizener admit only the last and title story as relevant: in Mizener's words, "His first use of it occurs in a story he wrote for the Josephine series just when he was beginning to grasp what had happened to Zelda; the story is called "Emotional Bankruptcy."[4] Eble reiterates this when he states that the same story "introduced the concept of 'emotional bankruptcy' which Fitzgerald felt was so applicable to his own life."[5]

But what happens to Josephine in *this* story can best be understood if we have seen what has happened in the first four stories, for aside from his letters to his daughter, it is in the Josephine stories *collectively* that he defines the state and examines the causes of "emotional bankruptcy." Josephine Perry is at once an individual, a representative of at least two generations, and, finally, a representative of the kind of person with a romantic sensibility that could lead to the emotional bankruptcy of an Anthony Patch, a Dick Diver, or a Monroe Starr.

Due to the circumstances of publication and the previous misreading of the stories, however, their nature and significance have been neglected. Because they were originally published in *The Saturday Evening Post* over a period of about a year and a half (between April 1930 and August 1931)[6] and because "Emotional Bankruptcy," the last and most obvious of the stories, was not published until nine months after the fourth Josephine story, they were not viewed as a whole in which the gradual emotional destruction of a character was depicted. In addition to this—perhaps because of it—no critical attention was given the stories until three of them were collected in *Taps at Reveille* in 1935, a collection from which "Emotional Bankruptcy" was omitted, thus helping to prevent the important linkage of the first four stories to the bankruptcy theme. The few reviews which did give specific mention to the collected ones frequently criticized them as "dated," or else the characterization of Josephine was judged against—and found inferior to—the warm, individual creation achieved in the Basil Duke

Lee group which immediately preceded the Josephine stories in the book.[7]

Both of these criticisms, however, indicated—and perhaps led future readers to—a misreading of the Josephine stories. In the first place, Josephine Perry is not only an individual—she is, as Fitzgerald described her in the very first story of the series and as will be demonstrated, "a pioneer of the generation that was destined to get out of hand."[8] To Fitzgerald she was the allegorical beginning of a whole American generation which had become emotionally bankrupt through its own waste and extravagance in the Twenties and which he feared still existed in the Thirties when he wrote the stories. Fitzgerald, who later admitted that he was "too much of a moralist at heart and really want[ed] to preach at people in some acceptable form rather than to entertain them,"[9] had carefully set Josephine up as a representative.

He had begun by "dating" her—by setting the stories between 1914 and 1917—even though as a successful popular writer he must have known that he could have made them more commercial by altering styles and changing dates. But 1914 was the beginning of the restless generation and the social changes which were soon reflected in the beginning of the war, and Josephine was, as Fitzgerald expressed it in the fourth story, "impatient for a change"; she was "representing in her own person the future."[10]

Then, in order to emphasize the change, he proceeded, in every story, to play her off against the behavior and standards of the previous generations represented both by her parents and her sister. Fitzgerald was allegorically depicting in Josephine (in spite of her basis in Ginevra King, the aristocratic beauty who rejected him) the menace of emotional bankruptcy brought about by the premature adventure, self-indulgence, and justification of sins referred to in one of Fitzgerald's most frequently quoted letters to Scottie: "For premature adventure one pays an atrocious price .... It's in the logic of life that no young

7

person ever 'gets away with anything.' . . . It was in the cards that Ginevra King should get fired from Westover—and that your mother should wear out young. I think that despite a tendency to self indulgence you and I have some essential seriousness that will manage to preserve us. Whatever your sins are I hope you never get to justify them to yourself."[11]

The old-fashioned morality of Josephine's family—the morality which Fitzgerald himself clung to, preached to Scottie, and continually presented in the stories—provided the necessary contrast to Josephine's violation of the old standards, and thus pointed up her sins more clearly. Her father's faithfulness to her mother in "A Snobbish Story" is an ideal which even Josephine cannot take lightly; her sister's friend in "First Blood" is a "reproachless bride, unsullied, beloved and holy with a sweet glow";[12] her sister is an equally reproachless bride. Then there are girls of Josephine's own generation, many of whom, like Adele Craw, "a pretty girl with clear honorable eyes and piano legs,"[13] still regard a kiss to be a proposal, or at least a promise. But Fitzgerald makes it clear even in the first story that the old standards are coming to an end: when her sister's friend marries "it was a sad and sentimental wedding—an end to the fine, glamourous youth of a girl who was universally admired and loved. Perhaps to no onlooker there were its details symbolical of the end of a period, yet from the vantage point of a decade, certain things that happened are already powdered with yesterday's ridiculousness, and even tinted with the lavender of the day before."[14] And it was no accident that Fitzgerald should, in the next story, describe the sister's wedding in which Josephine was maid of honor as "a lovely, sad wedding; the two sisters, light and dark, were a lovely contrast; there was as much interest in one as in the other."[15] For while her sister stood for the irreproachable, Josephine, with her dark head "demurely bowed . . . stood for the radiant future"[16] in the eyes of the sentimental congregation. But in reality she was soon to receive the kind of interest that the flapper received in the Twenties: she was, in fact, the forerunner of the Twenties and what Fitzgerald feared was the youth of the Thirties and might be that of the Forties. As a result of his fear, Fitzgerald set about systematically presenting the dangers and what he saw to be the inevitable end of such youthful self-indulgence in his portrayal of Josephine Perry's self-destruction. The Josephine stories, then, represent the bankruptcy of two generations and possibly a third.

Yet at the same time they present a thorough examination of the causes and course of emotional bankruptcy. In Josephine—and later in men like Anthony Patch and Dick Diver—self-indulgence, premature or otherwise, is closely linked to a romantic sensibility. This sensibility becomes a basis for the self-indulgence, and as he points up the unsuspecting self-destructive romanticism Fitzgerald carefully presents the other causes, spreading the destruction over a series of stories to let it take place gradually, in accordance with his conception of the ravages of emotional bankruptcy. From "First Blood" to "Emotional Bankruptcy," the pattern is clearly depicted: Josephine moves from romantic self-indulgence and premature adventure to their inevitable end—the inability to feel not only real love or even the sense of adventure, but *any*thing.

"First Blood" seems to begin innocently enough when sixteen year-old Josephine rejects her current "lover" because "the romantic mystery of the world had moved into another man."[17] Parroting virtuous Ed Bement in terms which reflect the bankruptcy theory, she informs Travis de Coppet that "I've decided not to kiss any more boys, because I won't have anything left to give the man I really love"—and then begins her pursuit of Anthony Harker. Finally, discovering that to Anthony she is a potential bride and not merely an "adventure," Josephine "repents" and rejects him. But as Fitzgerald had pointed out during one of her earlier moments of repentence, "Josephine knew that she only wanted to want such wants for her soul's sake. Actually, she had no desire for achievement. Her grandfather had had that, her parents had had the consciousness of it," but Josephine is one of the useless people that Fitzgerald condemns. Like the Puritans and Josephine's grandfather, Fitzgerald seems to equate morality with hard work and a sense of purpose and immorality with frivolity and extravagence. For him, the passing of the old standards means destruction, and in reading the stories it is important that we recognize that in theme, if not always in art, they are more than the typical *Post* plot stories.

In the second story, "A Nice Quiet Place," Josephine, whose entanglements have become much-talked-about, is sentenced to "a nice quiet place" for the summer, and her romanticism becomes desperate: "She could have cared for almost anyone. She wanted to hear the mystical terminology of love, to feel the lift and pull inside herself that each one of a dozen affairs had given her."[18] Finding an unexpected possibility in Sonny Dorrance, a sought-after young man seeking to escape his popularity, she denounces the "immorality" of Lake Forest, preferring to remain in her "nice quiet place."

But her wasted emotions have begun to take their toll, and in the next story Fitzgerald has made the consequences quite clear to his readers, although it is not until two stories later that it becomes completely clear to Josephine. "A Woman with a Past" contains Fitzgerald's most unsentimental and artistic depiction of Josephine's impending and inevitable bankruptcy, and perhaps this is why Fitzgerald chose to conclude the collected series with this story instead of the more obvious, but "Posty," one bearing the name of the theory. At any rate, he opens the story with Josephine anticipating her first Yale prom and finding herself "surprisingly unmoved" and disillusioned: "She was exactly seventeen and she was blasé . . . . She had grown bored with the waning September days—and it seemed as though it had happened once too often."[19] Worried by her indifference, bored with her own escort, and intrigued by Adele Crow's old-fashioned ideals, she becomes curious about Adele's popular but upright escort. In her pursuit and first defeat, she learns that "there were two kinds of men, those you played with and those you might marry," and she decides not to play with one particularly eligible young man. But she cannot give up playing altogether, and so when the other kind asks her to leave the dance and "walk out with him into the night"—a phrase evoking an almost symbolic meaning—she not only goes, but she goes "with a certain sense of relaxation." The bankruptcy is well on its way; it needs only the final proof and recognition.

The fourth story, however, holds off the recognition temporarily, perhaps in an effort to prolong a source of commercial success. In "A Snobbish Story" Josephine, who has "developed early and lived hard . . . and . . . begun to find men less than satisfactory,"[20] is allowed to follow her "call to adventure" into the only place left for her—the "sordid" world of the handsome but poor—and married—John Bailey. Finding in it a purposeful romanticism, but real passions and emotions which she is incapable of, she retreats back to her world of wealth and glamorous games until Fitzgerald presents her with the knowledge of her bankruptcy in the final Josephine story—the one which appeared nine months later and bears the name of the theme which had been central to the series.

When "Emotional Bankruptcy" opens, Josephine is just one month short of eighteen, the age at which she is, significantly, to make her debut—her official entrance into "society" and all its excitement and gayety. But Josephine has already been very much a member of society for two years, and her second prom proves dull and unreal. During a romantic interlude with a man she has set out to win over, she is bored. For those who haven't read the earlier stories, Fitzgerald explains: "It had been like that for almost a year—a game played with technical mastery, but with the fire and enthusiasm gone."[21] This, however, and the weekend which fails to excite her are merely "set-ups" for the final scene in which Josephine has met the man whom she believes could fulfill her, and after long anticipation she is given a kiss and a proposal. They kiss; they kiss again, and when he asks, she is honest: "I feel nothing at all . . . . You're everything I've always wanted . . . but I've had everything." The senti-

11

mental scene concludes with her realizing Fitzgerald's thesis "that all the old things are true. One cannot both spend and have. The love of her life had come by, and looking in her empty basket, she had found not a flower left for him—not one." And so we leave her crying "What have I done to myself? . . . What have I done?"

Unfortunately the story is artistically bad—it contains an obvious commercial triteness and melodramatic appeal which has caused too many critics to pass it off as *Saturday Evening Post sentiment*" when it is actually much more than that, as "A Woman with a Past" demonstrated more satisfactorily. Later, in 1939, Fitzgerald again expressed the dangers of his theory for both the young—like Josephine and Scottie, and for himself: "Our danger is imagining that we have resources—material and moral—which we haven't got . . . . Do you know what bankruptcy exactly means? It means drawing on resources which one does not possess . . . . Wiser people seem to manage to pile up a reserve . . . but I think that, like me, you will be something of a fool in that regard all your life . . . ."[22]

Certainly Josephine was a "fool in that regard," but there are others in Fitzgerald's work, as the best critics have pointed out, who imagined that they had—or never imagined they hadn't—resources which they did not possess. They can be found in *The Beautiful and the Damned, The Great Gatsby, The Last Tycoon, The Crack Up,* and such additional stories as "One Trip Abroad," and "Babylon Revisited," and we can best understand them and their sickness if we have understood Josephine first, for it is through her that we are shown in detail that a romantic sensibility coupled with self-indulgence will lead to wasted emotions until there are no more to waste.

Ohio State University

---

[1] Mizener, (Boston: Houghton Mifflin, 1965), p. 74.

[2] Mizener; Lehan, *F. Scott Fitzgerald and the Craft of Fiction* (Carbondale and Edwardsville: Southern Illinois University Press, 1966); Eble, *F. Scott Fitzgerald: A Critical Portrait* (New York: Twayne, 1965).

[3] Lehan and Piper.

[4] Mizener, p. 272.

[5] Eble, p. 118.

[6] The original chronology and publication dates are as follows:

"First Blood," CCII, April 5, 1930.

"A Nice Quiet Place," CCII, May 31, 1930.

"A Woman with a Past," CCIII, September 6, 1930.

"A Snobbish Story," CCIII, November 29, 1930.

"Emotional Bankruptcy," CCIV, August 15, 1931.

[7] For summaries of reviews of *Taps*, major and minor, see Jackson Bryer, *The Critical Reputation of F. Scott Fitzgerald: A Bibliographical Study* (Hamden, Connecticut: Archon Books, 1967).

[8] "First Blood," *Taps at Reveille* (New York: Scribners, 1935), p. 134. References to the uncollected stories are to the *Post* appearances. All other references are to *Taps at Reveille* as cited above. Collation of these with the *Post* versions indicates no substantive variants in the passages cited.

[9] *The Letters of F. Scott Fitzgerald,* ed. Andrew Turnbull (New York: Scribners, 1963), Letter to Scottie, November 4, 1939, p. 63. All letters cited were written to Scottie and published in this edition.

[10] "A Snobbish Story," *Post*, 6.

[11] July 5, 1937, Turnbull, pp. 15-16.

[12] p. 150.

[13] "A Woman with a Past," *Taps*, p. 178.

[14] "First Blood," *Taps*, pp. 148-149.

[15] "A Nice Quiet Place," *Taps*, p. 176.

[16] *Ibid.*

[17] *Taps*, p. 137.

[18] "A Nice Quiet Place," *Taps*, p. 158.

[19] "A Woman with a Past," *Taps*, p. 178.

[20] "A Snobbish Story," *Post*, 36.

[21] "Emotional Bankruptcy," *Post*, 9.

[22] April 5, 1939, Turnbull, p. 55.

Hollywood—It Wasn't All That Bad

By

R. L. Samsell

F. Scott Fitzgerald's picture looks down on me. I frown. He smiles. What I want—truly want—is to become a dead and forgotten darling the way he was when he hit Hollywood in July of 1937. What a pathetic, shy, battered ol' failure. Just pluggin' along at one thousand per week, suffering six months to get that mere raise to twelve-fifty. What a struggle. Those were inflation days, too. A dollar hardly went anywhere. He sure had it tough, Ol' Scott.

Think of the decisions he had to make? Let's see—"Should I go to the Troc, or The Players? Hey, Sheilo, let's have dinner at Musso & Franks."

There were the book stores, too. Stanley Rose's was the best, the friendliest. "Maybe we'll see Pep West there. Okay?"

Of course, his friends weren't much. And they were dull as hell—Robert Benchley, Charlie Butterworth, John O'Hara, Nunnally Johnson, Dorothy Parker. Sure, just run o'the mill.

Then, too, should he write another Pat Hobby story, or was it time to get at the new, big, gorgeous novel? Oh, it must've been tough, all right. Should he send Scottie to Europe that summer of '38? What about Vassar? That's not a bad school. Should they go to Norma Shearer's party? Pep, he's having a

15

party, too. But where was the time to write to John Biggs, S. J. Perelman, Arnold Gingrich, Thomas Wolfe, Helen Hayes, Gerald Murphy, Edmund Wilson, Budd Schulberg, Max Perkins, Ernest Hemingway? As Pearl Bailey used to sing—"That's not a bad bunch to hang out with."

Then there were the practical problems. Like moving from the Garden of Allah to the beach house at Malibu. Did Allah's bungalow actually cost four-hundred dollars per month? At Malibu, though, they could afford a servant. Later, at Horton's Belly Acres, they could afford a secretary for work on the novel. Finally, the apartment on North Laurel Avenue was, and is, an attractive, imposing structure.

Occasionally, away from the writing, there was time to take in the town, to root for U.C.L.A. at the Coliseum, to talk with Bogart at The Players, to hold sway with Thomas Mann when the latter appeared from his Santa Monica retreat.

And the writing was going great there toward the end. Perhaps it was going too well. Free of the movies, he was writing day in, day out, in or out of bed, writing stories as well as the more exacting work on *The Last Tycoon*. Already, Scribners and *Collier's* were interested in the novel, and, effervescing, he wrote to his daughter that he was working on something that was very dear to him.

Whatever his health was, or was not, it seems clear that even he was not aware of its ultimate, or terminal, seriousness. He was drinking Cokes, eating chocolate bars, right up to the end, and it was not uncommon for him to stroll around the neighborhood, occasionally walking up to Schwab's for this or that, perhaps only for the newspaper. The very night before his death, he and Miss Graham had taken in a movie at the Pantages in Hollywood. But perhaps his work-product attests to the energies his health allowed him to expend. Within one year of Scott Fitzgerald's death, Scribners published a handsome volume of the fragmentary *Tycoon*, while, also, and significantly, there were published nine stories within that same year. In all, during those forty-one months of his last Hollywood stint, Fitzgerald's discipline accomplished the eventual publication—either during those months or subsequently—of more than thirty stories and articles. It is meaningful to note that the Pat Hobby characterization warranted a seemingly endless series in one of America's finest magazines.

In a word, I feel too much has been made of Fitzgerald's difficulties in Hollywood. His experiences with 'story conferences' were just the kind of bludgeoning all writers endured. His poor health, too, has been sorely dramatized. He was still doing the town, attending select parties right up to the end. Local book dealers recall him well. I could name a half-dozen or so oldtimers who saw and talked with him often. One biographer suggests there was depression in the ". . . flat, drugstore sprawl of Los Angeles with its unnatural glaring sun." Another biographer tells us that Fitzgerald ". . . tired easily and didn't have enough energy to devote a full day to writing, . . . " But what exacting writer does? The point is this: Scott Fitzgerald was a well-organized, highly trained, and disciplined spirit who knew how to live better than most. In those last months, he was studying art, music, building a solid reading library. His dreams were intact. His talent was at or near its peak. Ironically, there have been those who have remarked sadly upon his last few years, although, by whatever standards, these same mourners never accomplished in their lifetimes what he generated in just those same, brief years.

Perhaps one of our scholars will one day inquire, seriously, of how much time and emotion F. Scott Fitzgerald poured into the grateful attentions of others. Wherever he paused in the sprawling, sun-glaring town, he left someone with a touch of his special stardust—his caring, or humor, his spirit of generosity. When he promised an acquaintance he would send inscribed copies of his novels, the novels arrived in an orange crate, jammed, fully, with books he wished the acquaintance to read. And the promised inscriptions were not the trite phrases of the usual author. Indeed, a compilation of Fitzgerald's inscriptions would be, in themselves, literature of a special kind of merry thoughtfulness. They still show up around town. I proudly shelve a *Gatsby* in which he prefaces his humor by affixing an appropriate magazine blurb with two band-aids. You see, in those difficult Hollywood days, he had been slapped by a Scandinavian beauty. Recently, a Beverly Hills dealer offered me a four-line poem for $400.00—merely a humorous chiding of the fan's request for Fitzgerald's autograph, when, forsooth, the fan had failed to send a return postage stamp. Then, obliging, the poem was followed by Fitzgerald's signature, covering more than five full inches of the page.

Then, too, Scott Fitzgerald could not settle for the usual greeting card. It was during those Hollywood days he sent the following Valentine to an old friend in the East:

> Valentine was a Saint;
> He was all I ain't.
> That's why he was blessed
> Along with all the rest
> Of them Holy birds
> Spoutin' joyful words.
>
> I wish I was a Saint
> Anyway what I ain't
> Then I could be right with you.
> Gee, oh golly, how I mith you.
>
> HAPPY VALENTINE

Oh, he had heart trouble, all right. His heart was just too damned big.

Zelda Fitzgerald knew better than anyone the nature of the man, when, writing after his death, she said, "He was as spiritually generous a soul as ever was . . . ." And by whatever standards, other than fiscal, Fitzgerald died a strong success. Nor was his greatness overlooked. He knew full well the authorities were in the wings, as, indeed, in the *New Republic*, 1941, they so stoutly appeared.

18

So when you think of Fitzgerald in Hollywood, try to see him in the light of hard work, of good times, friends of his own selection, places of his own liking, moments that were probably among his best. Ironically, except when we read about Fitzgerald, we hear of Hollywood in the Thirties as perhaps its true, golden age. He enjoyed some of that aura. Be sure of it. You and I should have known such times. You and I should do so well.

Zelda Fitzgerald. Untitled gouache. 25 1/2″ × 19″. Collection of
Matthew J. Bruccoli.

The Vogue of Gatsby's Guest List

By

Robert Emmet Long

The guest list device in *The Great Gatsby* has often been sin-
gled out for praise; when Maxwell Perkins read the manuscript
of the novel, for example, he wrote to Fitzgerald of "the mar-
velous catalogue of those who came to Gatsby's house—these
are such things as make a man famous."[1] The guest list is in
thumbnail form a summary of the twenties era; the sense of a
distinctive place and era is captured in the parade of grotesque
names of guests and in incidental comment revealing their aim-
less and mismanaged lives. Doctor Webster Civet, the Horn-
beams and the Willie Voltaires, Edgar Beaver, Ripley Snell
(whose hand was run over one night by the automobile of
Mrs. Ulysses Swett as he crawled intoxicated across a gravel
drive), S. W. Belcher, the Smirkes, and Henry L. Palmetto (who
killed himself by jumping in front of a subway train in Times
Square)—all of these figures condense into two pages the whole
bizarre ambiance of Gatsby's life on Long Island.[2]

Admiration of the guest list, however, has not been confined
to critics; since the beginning of the Fitzgerald revival, the device has been emulated by a later generation of creative writers—
conspicuously by William Styron in his novel *Lie Down in
Darkness.* The decadent affluence of the country club life

Styron describes in his novel evokes at times the tone and style of Fitzgerald; but his "guest list" of the country club set is, in particular, strikingly indebted to Fitzgerald in the coupling of grotesque names and fates:

There were the Appletons and the La Farges and the Fauntleroy Mayos, who were F.F.V.'s; and the Martin Braunsteins, who were Jews, but who had been around long enough to be accepted as Virginians. Then there was a contingent of doctors and their wives—Doctors . . . J. E. B. Stuart and Lonergan and Bulwinkle (they all smelled faintly of ether)—and there was Dr. Pruitt Delaplane, making his first hesitant public appearance after his trial and acquittal for criminal abortion. There were poor Medwick Ames and his wife—who threw fits . . .

Among the younger people were the Walker Stuarts and the P. Moncure Yourtees and George and Gerda Rhoades, who were, everyone knew, on the verge of divorce, and a man's clothing dealer named "Cherry" Pye. The Blevinses had come, and the Cappses and John J. Maloneys. Also the Davises and the Younghusbands and the Hill Massies, who had once won ten thousand dollars in a slogan contest; and a dentist named Monroe Hobbie, who limped . . .[3]

Even more recently, in James Baldwin's novel *Tell Me How Long the Train's Been Gone,* there is a guest list device which attempts to do for contemporary Greenwich Village what Fitzgerald did for the fictional West Egg of the twenties. Fitzgerald's language ("there came . . . there came") is echoed in Baldwin. Fitzgerald writes: "From East Egg, then, came the Beckers and the Leeches . . . . The Dancies came, too, and S. B. Whitebait . . . . From West Egg came the Poles and the Mulreadys . . . . All these people came to Gatsby's house in the summer." Baldwin uses the same method of introduction to give a capsule resume of strange and confused lives:

Here they came: the nice blonde girl from Minneapolis, who lived in the Village with her black musician husband. Eventually he went mad and she turned into a lush . . . . Here they came: the black man from Kentucky, who called himself an African prince and had some ridiculous name, like Omar, and his trembling Bryn Mawr girl-friend, whose virginity he wore like a flag . . . . here they came, the beautiful girl who painted and who ended up in prison . . . . Yes, my days of anger.[4]

Baldwin's "guest list" presentation of life at a bohemian and racially mixed Village restaurant forms, whether intentionally or not, an extension of the guest list device in *The Great Gatsby;* Styron's "guest list" in *Lie Down in Darkness* seems even more definitely modeled after Fitzgerald. The two taken together indicate the extent to which Gatsby's guest list is becoming a literary vogue. This vogue is not only a tribute to the evocative power of the guest list passage; it also illustrates that Fitzgerald laid claim to a particular territory of the imagination so that writers today, attempting something similar, are impelled back to Fitzgerald as their authority.

Queens College, CUNY

---

[1] Maxwell Perkins, *Editor to Author* (New York: Scribners, 1950), p. 41.
[2] The guest list appears pp. 73-76 of the first printing.
[3] *Lie Down in Darkness* (New York: Bobbs-Merrill, 1951), p. 261.
[4] *Tell Me How Long the Train's Been Gone* (New York: Dial Press, 1968), pp. 372-373.

The Great Gatsby and *Heart of Darkness:* The Confrontation Scenes

By

Harold Hurwitz

It has long been known that Joseph Conrad exerted a strong influence on F. Scott Fitzgerald's work. Statements of his debt to the English novelist appear frequently in Fitzgerald's letters, the most direct occurring in a note to H. L. Mencken written shortly after *The Great Gatsby* was published. "By the way, you mention in your review of *Sea Horses* that Conrad has only two imitators," he wrote. "How about . . . Me in *Gatsby* (God! I've learned a lot from him) . . . ."[1]

Several recent studies have attempted to define what Fitzgerald imitated and what he learned. The earliest of these was R. W. Stallman's essay on "Conrad and *The Great Gatsby*," which pointed out the parallels between Fitzgerald's novel and *Nostromo*, *Lord Jim*, and *Heart of Darkness*.[2] Later, Jerome Thale shed further light on this problem in his discussion of the similarity in structure between *Gatsby* and Conrad's work.[3] Most recently, R. E. Long's two-part essay in *Texas Studies* offers a great deal of evidence for Fitzgerald's indebtedness to Conrad's early work, including *Heart of Darkness*, in the organization of *Gatsby*.[4] In addition, most of the books on Fitzgerald have dealt with the influence problem.[5]

But no one, to my knowledge, has commented in detail upon

the similarities between the interview scenes occurring at the end of *Gatsby* and *Heart of Darkness*. Although Long rightly remarks that these episodes are used to emphasize the illusions of the heroes and the naiveté of the commentators, he finds that the parallels between them, although "conspicuous," are important only as similarities in detail.[6] However, it seems to me that the confrontation scene in *Gatsby* is a particularly important correspondence, for it is the one episode in it which in form and content is most clearly patterned after a scene in *Heart of Darkness*; and, as such, not only verifies Fitzgerald's debt to this work, but shows what he found useful in Conrad. Also, a close study of the changes Fitzgerald made helps to illuminate the fundamental difference between the two books.

In both, the narrators, Nick Carraway and Marlow, are faced with the difficult task of trying to tell the truth about complex characters (Gatsby and Kurtz) to listeners who are laboring under severe illusions about them. The narrators' difficulty is further compounded by the fact that they themselves do not have a clear picture of the men they are describing. Marlow keeps thinking of Kurtz as a "shadow;" and Nick, late in the story, suggests that Gatsby's life, like his house, was an "incoherent failure." Furthermore, both Mr. Gatz and Kurtz's fiancée are emotionally tied to their heroes, so that Nick and Marlow must tread softly.

Carraway and Marlow are thus involved in situations colored by a two-fold irony: on one side is the difference between appearance and reality, and on the other is the futility of truthfulness. Fitzgerald and Conrad underscore the irony in these scenes. As Marlow listens to the young lady's praise of Kurtz, he recalls the latter's barbarity and, especially, his final indictment of himself and the life he led: "The horror! The horror!" Likewise, Nick is forced to endure Mr. Gatz's praise of his son, although Nick knows that Gatsby was a racketeer. Carraway is particularly aware of Gatsby's dishonesty at the time he is talking to Mr. Gatz, for shortly before the latter appeared, Nick had spoken on the telephone to Slagle, one of Gatsby's associates, who, mistakenly taking Nick for Gatsby, had informed him that one of their accomplices was in trouble for passing falsified bonds: "They picked him up when he handed the bonds over the counter," Slagle tells Nick. "They got a circular from New York giving 'em the number just five minutes before. What d' you know about that, hey?" Thus, both narrators find themselves with a dilemma, in the face of which they are almost helpless.

In addition, the structure and progression of Fitzgerald's dialogue are similar to Conrad's. Firstly, Mr. Gatz, like Kurtz's intended, seeks to discover the closeness of the relationship between the narrator and the departed. The fiancée is seeking corraboration; Gatz, sympathy: "You knew him well," says the intended. "Were you a friend of my boy's, Mr. _____?" asks Gatsby's father.

After getting affirmative replies, the bereaved seek to impress their confidantes with the nobility of their lost ones: "It was impossible to know and not to admire him. Was it?" she asks. "He had a big future before him, you know," says Mr. Gatz. "He was only a young man, but he had a lot of brain power here." The rest of the interview scenes in both novels turn into apotheoses of the heroes by the speakers, followed by ambiguous or noncommittal replies by the narrators.

However, there are important differences. In the first place, Marlow plays a more active role in the dialogue than Carraway. Although he does not contradict Kurtz's fiancée, he answers her with such ambiguity that he is successful in preserving some of his integrity. Marlow realizes that the young lady is misinterpreting his responses; but they are misunderstandings on her part, not lies on his (except for his account of Kurtz's last words). For example, in speaking of his death, the fiancée remarks that "he died as he lived." Marlow answers evasively that "his end . . . was in every way worthy of his life."

Furthermore, Marlow is emotionally involved in the exchange. As he listens to the fiancée's praise of Kurtz, he becomes increasingly despondent. His mood is reflected in the sombre images that color the last pages of the novel, images suggesting the darkness of her ignorance, the depth of Marlow's despair over it, his awareness of the futility of trying to explain, and the gloomy impact of Kurtz's last words. Besides depression, Marlow experiences anger and fright during their conversation.

Carraway's role is more passive. He rarely employs irony with Mr. Gatz, he seems unmoved by the latter's remarks, and Fitzgerald doesn't use imagery to underline the importance of the dialogue. Carraway either nods in agreement or fails to make any reply.

There are also differences in the authors' attitude toward and their treatment of the bereaved. The fiancée is beautiful and dignified, and Marlow treats her with respect. The stature of Kurtz's intended is indicated by the appointments of the room in which she receives Marlow. Her drawing room, he says, was a "lofty" one, and had a "tall marble fireplace." Later, he notices a grand piano, which he describes as standing "massively" in a corner. The solidity of the furnishings supports his ironic comment on "her mature capacity for fidelity, for belief, for suffering."

In describing Mr. Gatz, Fitzgerald consciously employs Conrad's technique of choosing only those details that will "make you see;"[7] but Gatz, unlike the fiancée, is vulgar and banal. This is revealed in Carraway's description of the old man, who is introduced to us as being "helpless and dismayed, bundled up in a long cheap ulster against the warm September day." The weakness of his character is further disclosed in his "leaking eyes" and the sparsity of his grey beard.

The dissimilarities in these scenes can be explained not only by the differences in the character of the confidantes, but also by the degree of involvment the narrators have had with the dead legends. Marlow, for example, is much more committed to Kurtz than Nick is to Gatsby. This is partly due to the fact that Marlow's social position is closer to that of his protagonist. Marlow has been and is a ship's captain, with the power, privilege, and responsibility which that position confers. Kurtz was absolute master of the Inner Station.

Furthermore, Marlow has been subject to the same emotional pressures which Kurtz succumbed to. His sympathetic response to the shrieking of the natives on the way to the Inner Station makes him aware of the brutality in his own nature. In discovering Kurtz, he has realized some awful truths about man's savage propensities. He tells the fiancée a monstrous lie about Kurtz's last words as a final tribute to and acknowledgement of the ineradicable element of hypocrisy in his own nature. He owes Kurtz a debt for helping him to discover this truth.

In addition, Kurtz is not only a brute but a consummate one. Like an artist, Kurtz has ordered his material and given it a form and essence which corresponds to and reflects his vision of reality. Marlow seems to admire the artistic aspects of Kurtz's achievement, even though he is terrified by its implications. He refers to his degradation as "incredible" but "exalted." Thus he lies to the fiancée out of respect for Kurtz's integrity and consistency. Kurtz's stated goal was to "exterminate the brutes," and he has done just that.

Nick's social position and the circle he moves in are far different from Gatsby's. The latter is richer and older. Nick symbolically lives in a little, $80 per month house on the edge of Gatsby's "huge place," with a "partial view" of his neighbor's lawn. The social distance is firmly established and is reflected in the objective tone of the narrative and the dispassionate treatment of Mr. Gatz.

However, the irony of Marlow's finding a man much different from the one he expected apparently appealed to Fitzgerald, for Jay Gatsby is also not what he has seemed to be. Marlow expects to find a great man, but finds a completely corrupted one instead. Carraway suspects that Gatsby is a criminal, but is surprised to discover that he is a romantic idealist as well. Both authors use this reversal of expectations as subtle suggestions about human complexity.

The differences in the relationship between the narrators and the mourners underscore the varied purpose of each scene. The nobility of the fiancée is a contrast to the depravity of Kurtz; and the irony of the episode lies in her illusions about him and in her slavish devotion to his memory. Furthermore, her reluctance or inability to understand Kurtz is the culmination of a series of frustrations Marlow has experienced whenever he has tried to explain Kurtz. In this sense the interview scene is closely related to an earlier chapter, in which, Marlow, with equal futility, tries to describe Kurtz to his companions aboard the *Nellie*: " 'Absurd!' " he cried. " 'This is the worst of trying to tell . . . . Here you all are, each moored with two good addresses, like a hulk with two anchors, a butcher round one corner, a policeman round another, excellent appetites, and temperature normal—you hear—normal from year's end to year's end. And you say, Absurd! Absurd be—exploded! Absurd!' "

Conrad's last scene thus deepens the nature of the tragedy. Not only are we all like Kurtz, but those who know this must suffer in silence. Or as Marlow puts it to his friends on the yawl: " 'And there, don't you see? Your strength comes in, the faith in your ability for the digging of unostentatious holes to bury the stuff in . . . .' " Given this situation, the future is indeed bleak, for we are all doomed to repeat Kurtz's mistakes. Marlow was able to restrain himself, but it was the heaviest temptation he ever had. Kurtz, stronger than most, could not. The reasons for the sombre atmosphere of the confrontation scene are now apparent.

Fitzgerald's episode is equally important in the structure of his novel, for like Conrad, he uses his interview scene as both a climax and an anticlimax. It is anticlimactic because the father's ignorance of his son's character has been anticipated in the same lack of awareness shown by Gatsby's guests; it is climactic in that through the father we begin to understand the son. Thus, Mr. Gatz represents and embodies the vulgar materialism of our culture, and, as such, both he and what he represents are responsible for Gatsby's distorted values. Fitzgerald's changes serve to make his novel, unlike Conrad's, a social tragedy.

Fitzgerald also uses the old man as a means for introducing another subject for social criticism. During their conversation Mr. Gatz shows Nick a "ragged old copy" of a book that Gatsby had read during his childhood. On the back cover of it, Gatsby had set down a daily schedule for himself as well as a set of "*General Resolves*," which included the following:

> No wasting time at Shafters [or a name, indecipherable]
> No more smokeing or chewing
> Bath every other day
> Read one improving book or magazine per week
> Save $5.00 [crossed out] $3.00 per week
> Be better to parents

Gatsby is thus revealed to us as a boy who grew up with a firm belief in the "American Dream," the success-through-hard-work ideal basic to American life from Poor Richard to Horatio Alger. His corruption, his loneliness, and the indignities surrounding his death and funeral are Fitzgerald's ironic comments upon the unreality of the dream, and its harmfulness. Likewise, Gatsby's failure to win Daisy is Fitzgerald's means for emphasizing the futility of the formula.

It is unlikely that the similarities between these episodes are accidental. There is overwhelming evidence that Fitzgerald was very conscious of Conrad's technique during the composition of *Gatsby*. This can perhaps best be seen in the remarks he made to Charles C. Baldwin shortly after finishing the novel: "The writer," he said, "if he has any aspirations towards art, should try to convey the feel of his scenes, places and people directly— as Conrad does, as a few Americans (notably Willa Cather) are already trying to do."[8] The value of this comparison is that it not only shows what Fitzgerald was attempting, but how and why he used an important episode in *Heart of Darkness* to do it.

Windham College

---

[1] *The Letters of F. Scott Fitzgerald*, ed. Andrew Turnbull (New York: Scribners, 1965), p. 482. Turnbull dates the letter "May or June, 1925." In addition, *The Crack-Up* contains several of Fitzgerald's references to Conrad, including his oft-quoted remark, made in a letter to Edmund Wilson in 1922, that he wanted "some new way of using the great Conradian vitality" (p. 262.).

See also "F on Conrad," *Fitzgerald Newsletter*, #40 (Winter 1968), 14.

[2] *Twentieth Century Literature*, I (April 1955), 5-12.

[3] "The Narrator as Hero," *Twentieth Century Literature*, III (July 1957), 69-73.

[4] Robert Emmet Long, "*The Great Gatsby* and the Tradition of Joseph Conrad, Part I," *Texas Studies in Literature and Language*, VIII (Summer 1966), 257-276; Part II, VIII (Fall 1966), 407-422. Long notes that there are references in Fitzgerald's letters and manuscripts which indicate he had read *Heart of Darkness* by 1925.

[5] Most helpful for literary matters are James E. Miller's *The Fictional Technique of F. Scott Fitzgerald* (1957) and *F. Scott Fitzgerald: His Art and His Technique* (1964).

[6] Part II, pp. 413 and 418.

[7] Fitzgerald had reread Conrad's preface to *The Nigger of the Narcissus* just before beginning *Gatsby*. In 1933, he defined his debt to Conrad and to the preface in this manner: "These old mistakes are now only toys—and expensive ones at that—give them a toy's cupboard and then hurry back into the serious business of my profession. Joseph Conrad defined it more clearly, more vividly than any man of our time:

'My task is by the power of the written word to make you hear, to make you feel—it is, before all, to make you see'."("One Hundred False Starts," *Saturday Evening Post*, CCV [March 4, 1933], 66.)

[8] Quoted in Baldwin's *The Men Who Make Our Novels* (New York: Dodd, Mead, 1925), p. 167.

T. J. Eckleburg; "un dieu à l'américaine"

By

William F. Hall

The Goncourt Journals for 1861 contain the following passage:

> Parfois je pense qu'il viendra un jour, où les peuples modernes jouiront d'un dieu à l'américaine, d'un dieu qui aura été humainement, et sur lequel il y aura des témoignages de petits journaux: lequel dieu figurera dans les églises, son image non plus élastique et au gré de l'imagination des peintres, non plus flottante sur le voile de Véronique, mais arrêté dans un portrait en photographie . . . Oui, je me figure un dieu en photographie et qui portera des lunettes.
>
> Ce jour-là, la civilisation sera à son comble, et l'on verra à Venise des gondoles à vapeur.[1]

The resemblance between this passage and that which describes the eyes of T. J. Eckleburg in *The Great Gatsby* is striking. Whether the first passage is a source of the second must be left open to doubt but the stress in it on the spectacled God as a peculiarly American one is interesting in view of some other links between the novel and outside sources, that suggest an important theme in the novel that has been overlooked.

Tom Buchanan's comments on the "going to pieces" of civilisation are based on a book he describes as " 'The Rise of the Colored Empires' by this man Goddard . . . . The idea is that if we don't look out the whole white race will be . . . utterly submerged. It's all scientific stuff . . . . This idea is that we're Nordics . . ." The book Fitzgerald almost certainly had in mind here was Lothrop Stoddard's *The Rising Tide of Color Against White Supremacy*. The book was first published in 1920 and reprinted in 1923 with an introduction by Madison Grant. (This might account for the portmanteau name "Goddard") Both Grant and Stoddard were rabid racists; the only difference between them was one of approach. As Stoddard notes in his preface: "A lifelong student of biology, Mr. Grant approaches the subject along that line. My own avenue of approach being world-politics . . . ."[2]

Stoddard insists that the " 'Nordic' American stock" is in serious danger from three sources: from "colored" (by which he means mainly Asiatic) immigration, from the "migrations of lower human types," and from the "lurking spectre of miscegenation." He contends also that these dangers involve the corruption, confusion and swamping of the "Nordic American" ideals.

It seems clear enough that the attribution of these ideas in this extreme form to the "varnished brute" (the phrase is that of Henry James) Buchanan and the emphasis on the "Nordic" appearance of the debilitated Wilson ("he was a blond spiritless man, anaemic . . . his light blue eyes") suggest a corruption, in Fitzgerald's view, *within* "Nordic America" itself, even while the implicit comments on the "non-Nordic" new elements in American society (as in the list of grotesque names on Gatsby's guest list) suggest that, at least within the limits of this novel, these new elements have no positive new moral ideal or energy to provide.

The "cradle of the Nordic stock" is shown in the persons of Buchanan and Wilson, and in the symbolic projection of the Valley of the Ashes as corrupt and decadent, and it is so as a result of a deterioration within itself, as well as from the confusion of values introduced with the immigration of other "stock." Eckleburg's faceless bespectacled blue eyes and the land on which they stare are then a projection of this; fit symbols of what the original energy and meaning of the Nordic myth have become.

It is worthwhile to consider the final famous paragraph of the novel in the light of what has been said so far. This, for all the rhapsodic praise of its lyric quality, has had astonishingly little said about its meaning.

The passage relates most obviously and clearly to those sections of the novel in which the life of the Mid-west middle-class from which Nick came is given a high positive value as distinct from the lack of value in the East. It relates also however, in a way that makes its meaning clear, and that lends further meaning to the passages about the Mid-west, to one of the central conceptions of Crévecoeur's *Letters from an American Farmer;* a conception that was to become a central part of the 19th Century myth of the frontier:

> . . . whence came all these people? They are a mixture of English, Scotch, Irish, French, Dutch, Germans, and Swedes. From this promiscuous breed, that race now called Americans have arisen. The Eastern provinces must indeed be excepted, as being the unmixed descendants of Englishmen.

> Those who live near the sea, feed more on fish than on flesh and often encounter that boisterous element. This renders them more bold and enterprizing; this leads them to neglect the confined occupations of the land . . . . Those who inhabit the middle settlements . . . . Europe has no such class of men . . . . a great deal of sagacity . . . . Industry, good living, selfishness, litigiousness, country politics, the pride of freemen, religious indifference, are their characteristics. If you recede still farther from the sea, you will come into more modern settlements; they exhibit the same strong lineaments, in a ruder appearance. Religion seems to have still less influence and their manners are less improved.

> Now we arrive near the great woods, near the last inhabited dis-
> tricts . . . . These men appear to be no better than carnivorous
> animals of a superior rank.[3]

In Crévecoeur's conception the ideal state exists in the "mid-
dle settlements." "Near the sea" (and by sea I take him to
mean the Atlantic) there is distraction from settled order; just
as in the far west, on the frontier, there will for other reasons be
a lack of peace and order. It is in the "rolling fields of the republic," to use Fitzgerald's phrase, rather than in the east of the
Buchanans or in the West of Dan Cody that the American dream
is to be realized. It is in terms of Créveceour's passage that, in
my opinion, the splendid rhetoric of Fitzgerald's coda acquires
a very solid and significant meaning.

The original (and essentially pastoral) ideal of America dissi-
pated the instant European man set foot on the continent.
From that instant, paradoxically then, what all later generations
have regarded as future possibility has in fact been always nostalgia for a past that is (hence the boat image) ever receding
with our efforts to attain it. In the case of the individual (here
Nick Carraway) this is nostalgia for his own past (Nick's Mid-
western childhood) that becomes the image of an unrealizable
ideal after which he constantly strives. In the case of society a
nostalgic image of a perfectly simple Arcadia becomes the image
of an ideal towards which society tries constantly to move; an
ideal that must inevitably recede further into the past the more
complex and urbanised and rootless the society becomes.

The qualified optimism then of the final image — with its suggestions of constant effort, of guidance from the past, of an un-
known destination, of no sense of arrival but only of travelling
(and travailling) is the note on which the novel ends. It is one
that relates the novel's meaning to, on the one hand, the nine-
teenth century Transcendentalists, as well as to the ideals of
Pound and Eliot for both of whom:

> . . . right action is freedom
> From past and future also.

For most of us this is the aim
Never here to be realised;
Who are only undefeated
Because we have gone on trying;
We, content at the last

. . . . .

The life of significant soil.[4]

University of British Columbia

---

[1] Edmond et Jules de Goncourt, *Journal; Memoirs de la Vie Litteraire,* ed. Lucien Descaves (Paris, 1936) Vol. I, p. 306.

[2] Stoddard's book was first published in 1920 and reprinted in 1923. This is not, I assume, the same Stoddard whose bound lectures are taken from the shelves of Gatsby's library by Owl-Eyes. The lecturing Stoddard was John Lawson Stoddard whose highly popular travel lectures were collected in 1901 into fifteen volumes. Part of his fame as lecturer rested on his use of the stereopticon. This device produced the effect of one picture's dissolving while another was forming. Given the mention of Stoddard's books following immediately on the mention of Belasco (whose theatrical productions were noted for their convincing air of reality) it's possible that it was this fact about Stoddard that may have suggested the use of his volumes in this context. For Gatsby's "library" is as unreal as the whole persona he has created for himself.

[3] Hector St. John de Crévecoeur, *Letters from an American Farmer* intro. W. B. Blake (London, 1912), pp. 41-45.

[4] T. S. Eliot, "The Dry Salvages."

Scottie and F. Scott Fitzgerald. Collection of R. L. Samsell.

The Bibliography Of Fitzgerald's Magazine "Essays"

By

Roderick S. Speer

As the importance of F. Scott Fitzgerald's fiction increases in modern critical estimation, scholarship will turn for further insight to the considerable body of "non-fictional" prose he produced for magazines. The fame won in literature allowed Fitzgerald, as a celebrity of his time, to publish a variety of material not strictly literary. My purpose here is to indicate a general vagueness surrounding the classification of this material and to correct the errors in its bibliography. Since Jackson R. Bryer's *The Critical Reputation of F. Scott Fitzgerald: A Bibliographical Study* (Hamden: Archon, 1967) has become the indispensable handbook for Fitzgerald studies, my remarks will be addressed to correcting the errors in its Appendix "Checklist of the First Appearances of Publications Containing Items by Fitzgerald: II. Periodicals."

A vagueness surrounds the items not classified as "story." These items are called either "article" (Mizener and Porter) or, less fortunately, "essay" (Bryer). Many of these items, however, are in no sense compositions dealing with a particular subject, as we have come to regard an essay. Only the category "article" is neutral enough to include the varied kinds of contributions to magazines by FSF. Piper has drawn a more informative distinction between "Essays" and "Short Humorous Parodies, Sketches, and Dialogues." The following list is an example of items which I suggest do not belong in the category of "essay" as used by Bryer (and, in two cases, by Piper).[1]

1920 "This is a Magazine." Humorous sketch.

1923 "The Most Disgraceful Thing I Ever Did." Humorous anecdote.

1924 "The Cruise of the Rolling Junk." Humorous narrative.

1925 "My Old New England Homestead on the Erie." Parody story.

1929 "Ten Years in the Advertising Business." Satire. "A Short Autobiography (With Acknowledgements to Nathan)." Humorous sketch.

1930 "Salesmanship in the Champs-Élysées." Humorous dialogue.

1936 "Author's House"; "Afternoon of an Author." Quasi-autobiographical articles.

1937 "A Book of One's Own." Humorous sketch.

Other reclassifications may be demanded by different critical perspectives. It is important, though, to note the misleading simplicity of the dichotomy between story and essay, blinding us to the sketches, narratives, and *jeux d'esprit* occupying a middle-ground between them.

The following is an annotated list of errata in Bryer's listing of magazine "essay" material.

1920 "Who's Who—and Why," *Saturday Evening Post*, September 18. Omitted by Bryer.

1923 "The Most Disgraceful Thing I Ever Did." This item appears in the October *Vanity Fair*, not in November. Fitzgerald's unsigned contribution to the general heading is revealed in the January 1924 issue to have been No. 2, "The Invasion of the Sanctuary."

1924 "The Moment of Revolt that Comes to Every Married Man." The actual title is, "Does a Moment of Revolt Come Sometime to Every Married Man?"

"What Do We Wild Young People Want for Our Children," *Woman's Home Companion*, July. This title is not an actual one, nor is there any such essay. The entry probably refers to the FSF letter to the editor included on page 110 under "Who's Who in This Issue."

"The Flapper's Little Brother," *McCall's*, December. I have been unable to locate this article; it is apparently a ghost.

1925 "My Old New England Farm House on the Erie" is the Table of Contents title. The title over the article substitutes "Homestead" for "Farm House."

"What Becomes of Our Flappers and Sheiks?" is not a single article "written with Zelda Fitzgerald." It is the general heading for separate articles by each of the Fitzgeralds. Fitzgerald's is entitled "Our Young Rich Boys."

1928 "Looking Back Eight Years" . . ."(Written with Zelda Fitzgerald)." Piper notes from FSF's Ledger that this essay is completely by Zelda Fitzgerald.

"Who can Fall in Love after Thirty?" Bryer omits that this essay was signed by Zelda Fitzgerald as well. Piper notes again that it is completely by her.

1929 "A Short Autobiography." The title continues, "(With Acknowledgements to Nathan)."

1930 "Salesmanship on the Champs-Élysées." The actual title reads "in" for "on."

1934 "Show Mr. and Mrs. F. to Number–" and "Auction– Model 1934." Piper notes these articles are mostly by Zelda Fitzgerald.

1937 "A Book of My Own." The actual title reads "One's" for "My."

New entry:

1968 "My Generation." *Esquire*, October.

In Edmund Wilson's selection of Fitzgerald articles, *The Crack-Up*, there are bibliographical lapses. Wilson does not indicate the two 1934 articles, "Show Mr. and Mrs. F. to Number— " and "Auction—Model 1934" as being mostly by Zelda Fitzgerald. A more serious mistake is the reversal of the titles of the last two "Crack-Up" essays (although the body of these essays is presented in correct sequence). The correct sequence of titles is "The Crack-Up," "Pasting It Together," and "Handle With Care."

University of Pennsylvania

---

[1] There are three previous checklists of the magazine articles: Henry Dan Piper, "F. Scott Fitzgerald: A Checklist," *Princeton University Library Chronicle*, XII (Summer, 1951), 196–208; Arthur Mizener, "Fitzgerald's Published Work," in *The Far Side of Paradise* (Boston: Houghton, Mifflin, 1951; 2nd ed., 1965); and Bernard H. Porter, "The First Publications of F. Scott Fitzgerald," *Twentieth Century Literature*, V (January, 1960), 176–182. Mizener's is probably the best-known of these and unfortunately has been followed uncritically in almost every respect by both Porter and Bryer. Only Piper's checklist is accurate; Piper also goes beyond the magazine pieces dealt with here to newspaper and miscellaneous writings.

A Comparative Statistical Analysis Of The Prose Styles Of F. Scott Fitzgerald And Ernest Hemingway

By

Elizabeth Wells

Statistics supply the one asset in which literary criticism, especially stylistic criticism, has always been woefully deficient—proof. Numerical proof may never take the place of critical sensitivity, but by presenting good solid evidence, one can base his description and evaluation of an author's style on a good solid foundation that cannot be ignored by future critics who wish to escape into the never-never land of impressionistic criticism. In order to draw any meaningful conclusions from a statistical analysis, however, one must be prepared to relate the numbers and percentages of the specific sampling to corresponding numbers and percentages in additional samplings. This is the rationale and justification for a comparative analysis of the prose styles of F. Scott Fitzgerald and Ernest Hemingway.

The statistics have been taken from Fitzgerald's "The Rich Boy," parts I through V, and Hemingway's "Big Two-Hearted River: Part I." "Big Two-Hearted River" is early Hemingway. It is important to note here, however, that Hemingway was not a monolithic writer. In fact, his style changed over the years from the excessively clipped expression of *In Our Time* to the more mellow expression of *For Whom the Bell Tolls*. Moreover, within this gradual change, Hemingway experimented with rambling Faulknerian sentences in *Green Hills of Africa*. In brief, the progression from the style of *In Our Time* to the style of *For Whom the Bell Tolls* was a progression toward more complexity and variety in all matters except diction. The sentences became longer and grammatically more complex. More words were included inside dependent clauses. Sentence openers became more varied. Hemingway's diction, however, remained essentially of the same monosyllabic, Anglo-Saxon cast. On the other hand, Fitzgerald's style did not change appreciably from his first to his last story. Sentence structure and complexity of diction remained relatively stable. For specific statistics on brief selections from Hemingway's *For Whom the Bell Tolls* and *A Moveable Feast* and Fitzgerald's *Tender Is the Night* and *The Crack Up*, the reader is referred to the Appendix.

Having granted a difference in earlier and later Hemingway, I have chosen to describe in detail the most extreme example of the Hemingway style to be found in his earlier stories. For it was the earlier Hemingway that created a style that has since been copied and displayed as a model for a modern, no-nonsense, prose style. By describing the extreme, this study will be describing, therefore, those elements of his style that are most often identified with him and which earned him a reputation as one of the most conscientious stylists of American writers.

It may be argued that differing subject matter and point of view effects the reliability of comparative statistics. "The Rich Boy" is, after all, told by a narrator who has a personality of his own, whereas "Big Two-Hearted River" is told from an objective, third person point of view. In addition, Fitzgerald's story is about a man who is traveling in sophisticated, urbane society, while Hemingway depicts a man alone on a fishing trip for a day and a night. It would be a mistake, indeed, not to consider these matters of subject when the statistics are interpreted. A description of an author's style is, by implication, a description of his subject matter. Hemingway's fondness for simple diction is tied inextricably to the character of his male protagonists. Whenever necessary, therefore, forays will be made into the differing worlds of Nick Adams and Anson Hunter in order to interpret or qualify the statistics.

One very important limitation of this study, however, is the elimination of dialogue because the tools of statistical analysis do not readily lend themselves to work on dialogue. How does one classify a line like the following from "The Rich Boy:" "Cigarette? . . . Oh, I beg your pardon. By me." Is it one, two, or three sentences? Are the "sentences" to be considered fragments? Also, dialogue, by definition, consists of words spoken by a character and, ideally, reflects more upon that character's manner of speech than upon the author's prose style. Not much will be lost by ignoring the dialogue of the Hemingway story as there are only three short statements by Nick. Dialogue is liberally sprinkled throughout "The Rich Boy," however, and must be taken into account when one discusses paragraph length.

The length of a paragraph, the largest unit of written discourse, is determined by many considerations. Paragraphs written as lead-ins for dialogue will be shorter than most. But equally important is the subject matter of the paragraph, that is, whether the paragraph argues a point, provides descriptive background for future action, or describes action taking place over a time span of many years or a few minutes. The average paragraph length of "Big Two-Hearted River" is 105 words as opposed to only 77 words in "The Rich Boy," but the primary reason for this difference is the larger amount of dialogue in the "The Rich Boy." Significantly, three out of the six Hemingway paragraphs that fall under 35 words surround dialogue.

Paragraph length must not be counted out as an effective rhetorical device, however. The brevity of paragraph number five, the first short paragraph in "Big Two-Hearted River," is definitely used to highlight and intensify the action of that paragraph. After giving us four long paragraphs of strictly objective scene-setting in which Nick observes the ruins of Seney, Hemingway shifts to a very succinct statement of Nick's emotional reaction to the trout:

> Nick's heart tightened as the trout moved. He felt all the old feeling.

This paragraph is important. It is the first indication that Nick has returned to a world that means much to him, the first indication that this is not just another excursion. And the shift in cadence from the long descriptive paragraphs to this brief statement of emotion alerts the reader to its importance. Immediately following this first short paragraph is another short one that pictures Nick following the convolutions of the stream. Once again, this particular stream is very important; it is, in fact, the occasion for the title of the story.

Fitzgerald also used the device of short paragraphing to highlight important material. After giving an account of Anson's delay in asking Paula to marry him, the narrator states with blunt finality:

> He had forgotten that Paula too was worn away inside with the strain of three years. Her mood passed forever in the night.

This is a turning point in Anson's life and as such deserves to be set off and emphasized in one brief paragraph.

Unusually long paragraphs can also be used for effect. In the longest paragraph in the Hemingway story, 312 words, Nick is remembering something from his past. He is remembering Hopkins. The paragraph wanders as Nick's mind wanders. But Nick does not want to think; he wants to leave the past behind him for a while. And the long paragraph which describes Nick's lapse into the past is broken off only when he acts and drinks the coffee.

More important than any single lengthy paragraph in the

Fitzgerald selection are the patterns of paragraph length, that is, what portions of the story have consistently long paragraphs. It is not at all surprising that the paragraphs of section one, which constitute a rather argumentative introduction to the story, are all longer than the average length of 77 words in "The Rich Boy." Argumentation usually takes more words than straight description. Nor is it surprising that only one of the nine paragraphs of section two falls under the average. Here Fitzgerald is filling in Anson's background; he is covering a span of many years in each paragraph and this takes up space if it is to be done in any detail. None of section two achieves any immediacy. The narrator, in this section, is summing up the past in an orderly fashion. It is not until Anson becomes involved with Paula and the workings of their romance begin that the story starts to move. Contrast the shorter paragraphs beginning with paragraph number two of section three. The immediate action of Anson's unfortunate drunken spree, which covers a time span of one evening, is broken down and presented in more fragmented paragraphs. A quick glance at the beginning of section four will show that the pattern is being repeated. Again we are given summed-up past in longer-than-average paragraphs. Throughout the story Fitzgerald maintains this habit of shifting from longer paragraphs of orderly narrative exposition of events that cover long time spans to shorter paragraphs of fragmented description of immediate action that cover a single event.

No such pattern exists in the Hemingway story because the story takes place in one day and Nick Adams is given no past aside from the remembrance of Hopkins. On the surface, this distinction between Fitzgerald and Hemingway seems, at best, a statement of the obvious. But it does suggest something of significance about the way the two writers present a story. In almost every short story in the Fitzgerald canon, some biographical background is provided for the main characters. Furthermore, Fitzgerald almost always talks "about" his characters while he is presenting their actions. Hemingway, however, provides almost no biographical material in his short stories, especially in the Nick Adams stories which are small vignettes recounting an isolated event. And Hemingway seldom intrudes on his story to provide information about a character's personality. The relationship between subject matter and style, then, is of some importance when one considers paragraph length. Whereas Fitzgerald turns to longer paragraphing when he wishes to provide background for the action of the story, and then progresses to shorter paragraphs to describe that action, Hemingway, who provides no background, varies paragraph length for specific effects. Of the two styles, Hemingway's would have to be labeled more experimental.

The next largest unit of written discourse, the sentence, can be studied in terms of length, structure, and patterning. One would assume that since Hemingway's paragraphs are longer, his sentences are also longer than Fitzgerald's. But whereas Fitzgerald's sentences are by no means lengthy—the average is 24 words per sentence—Hemingway's sentences average exactly half as long. This statistic is even more striking in conjunction with the additional facts that while 20% of Fitzgerald's sentences are more than ten words over the average of twenty-four and 41% are five words or more below the average, only 12% of Hemingway's sentences are more than ten words over the average of twelve and 43% are five words or more below the average. This extreme divergence in sentence length can be accounted for by a coexistent divergence in degree of sentence complexity. Hemingway's sentences are short because 73% of them are simple sentences. Only 24% of Fitzgerald's sentences are simple. A full 61% of Fitzgerald's sentences are either complex or compound-complex as compared to only 25% for Hemingway. Traditionally Fitzgerald's style has been thought to be rather fluid and wandering, but statistics simply do not bear this out. Twenty-four words is not a long English sentence and 61% complexity is not extreme. In fact, it is interesting to note that these statistics for "The Rich Boy" come very close to approximating the comparable statistics from Hemingway's *For Whom the Bell Tolls* and *A Moveable Feast* in which the sentence lengths are respectively 21 words and 24 words and the degrees of complexity are respectively 48% and 66%. Yet, few critics would accuse Hemingway of being fluid and wandering, perhaps because they are so much under the influence of the style of his earlier works.

Clearly the extreme case here is Hemingway, and clearly his sentence brevity and simplicity is primarily confined to his earlier works. The immediate effect of such a style is obvious. It produces a choppy, Dick-and-Jane type of prose. The reasons for such writing are generally thought to be also very obvious. It is the paratactic syntax most often found among children who have not yet learned to subordinate their ideas and who, consequently, present ideas one after another without any relationships between them. It is most often considered to be the language of those incapable of cause-and-effect reasoning and unable to perform the more sophisticated mental activity of abstracting generalities out of specifics. But in Hemingway's case it is not a matter of being incapable of cause and effect reasoning and abstraction but of being unwilling to present either in this story. Although "Big Two-Hearted River" is told in the third person, we are never allowed to see more than Nick sees, and Nick, to repeat an earlier point, does not want to think. He wants to act. He is, in fact, consciously putting himself through a ritual that will keep him from thinking. Any complication, therefore, whether mental or linguistic, is, like the swamp, to be avoided. Possibilities abound for subordination in this story, but Hemingway refuses to take advantage of them. He writes, for example:

His muscles ached and the day was hot, but Nick felt happy. He felt he had left everything behind, the need for thinking, the need to write, other needs.

He could have written instead:

> Although his muscles ached and the day was hot, Nick felt happy
> because he felt he had left everything behind, the need for think-
> ing, the need to write, other needs.

Only once does Nick allow himself to search for causes and that
is when he examines the sooty grasshoppers. But there is little
danger in pondering the reason for grasshoppers turning black.
It is, however, important to note that the paragraph that describes Nick's puzzling over the grasshoppers contains more
subordinate clauses than any other paragraph in the story.

In direct contrast to Nick's self-imposed simplicity stands
the rather strained sophistication of the narrator of Fitzgerald's
"The Rich Boy." Here is a story-teller with a thesis to prove,
and he announces that thesis in the third paragraph of his
story:

> Let me tell you about the very rich. They are different from
> you and me. They possess and enjoy early, and it does something
> to them, makes them soft where we are hard, and cynical where we
> are trustful, in a way that, unless you were born rich, it is very diffi-
> cult to understand. They think, deep in their hearts, that they are
> better than we are because we had to discover the compensations
> and refuges of life for ourselves. Even when they enter deep into
> our world or sink below us, they still think that they are better than
> we are. They are different.

Fitzgerald's narrator is a man searching for causes, attempting
to understand a phenomenon that is outside of his realm of experience. No surprise, then, that his method of approach is so
much more complicated. First he must delve into Anson's past
to find some causes. Consider the sophisticated reasoning of
the following paragraph of five sentences, only one of which is
simple:

> Anson's first sense of his superiority came to him when he realized
> the half-grudging American deference that was paid to him in the
> Connecticut village. The parents of the boys he played with always

54

inquired after his father and mother, and were vaguely excited when their own children were asked to the Hunter's house. He accepted this as the natural state of things, and a sort of impatience with all groups of which he was not the centre—in money, in position, in authority—remained with him for the rest of his life. He disdained to struggle with other boys for precedence—he expected it to be given him freely and when it wasn't he withdrew into his family. His family was sufficient, for in the East money is still a somewhat feudal thing, a clan-forming thing. In the snobbish West, money separates families to form "sets."

The logic of sentence structure demands that subordination establish a clear scale of values by subordinating less worthy ideas into dependent clauses. In the Hemingway story little attempt is made to distinguish between the relative value of each of Nick Adams' ritual actions, whereas in the Fitzgerald story the narrator, by the very cast of his sentence structure, is constantly passing judgment on the facts and actions he presents. Only 15% of the Hemingway story is told inside dependent clauses as opposed to 35% of the Fitzgerald story.

Of equal significance is the type of dependent clause each author employs. Sixty-three percent of Hemingway's dependent clauses are adverbial and only six of those adverbial clauses are introduced by the subordinate conjunctions "since," "because," or "if," all of which establish causal relationship. Instead, Hemingway is fond of the subordinate conjunctions "as" and "while," which describe concurrent action. His longest sentence, in fact, contains three such clauses:

> *As the shadow of the kingfisher moved up the stream*, a big trout shot upstream in a long angle, only his shadow marking the angle, then lost his shadow *as he came through the surface of the water*, caught the sun, and then, *as he went back into the stream under the surface*, his shadow seemed to float down the stream with the current, unresisting, to his post under the bridge where he tightened facing up into the current.

When Hemingway wishes to express step-by-step action, he most often places one action after the other without any temporal connector. To provide the subordinate conjunctions "until" and "before" (he uses only five altogether) would be to needlessly complicate the sequential nature of the events. Sequence can be more easily and economically implied by placing one event after the other in successive sentences.

Fitzgerald, on the other hand, is not at all adverse to providing chronological connectors, and shows no such partiality to any type of clause. Twenty-eight percent of Fitzgerald's clauses are adjectival as compared to only 18% for Hemingway. The basic logic of an effective adjective clause is to put into many words what cannot be expressed adequately in one descriptive word. More words sometimes provide more detailed information but often simply provide more verbosity. Only occasionally, however, can Fitzgerald be accused of such verbosity. He could have said, for example, "A *new* note of tenderness ran through [her letters]" rather than saying "A note of tenderness ran through [her letters] *that had not been there before*." But little can be done to simplify the description "incongruities *which her gentle mind was unable to resolve*" without doing damage to the depth of descriptive power in the subordinate clause by replacing it with something much less satisfactory like "*unresolvable* incongruities."

When faced with a similar problem of description, Hemingway chooses repetition rather than subordination. Notice the repetition of the words "trees," "trunks," and "branches" in the following sentences:

> There was no underbrush in the island of pine *trees*. The *trunks* of the *trees* went straight up or slanted toward each other. The *trunks* were straight and brown without *branches*. The *branches* were high above.

Any two of these sentences could be combined by using adjectival subordinate clauses. For example, one could say, "The trunks, *which were straight and brown without branches*,

56

went straight up or slanted toward each other." This revision is certainly not an improvement and could only be justified on the basis of avoiding repetition and introducing sentence variety. But besides being one of the salient characteristics of the Hemingway style, repetition is essential to the ritual of this story.

Hemingway's fondness for repetition provides one of the most impressive differences between the Hemingway style and the Fitzgerald style; that is, whereas Fitzgerald's writing evidences no conscious attempt to pattern his words or phrases or sentences, Hemingway seldom fails to set up obvious patterns. Patterns may be created by repetition of the same key words, similar grammatical types of words, clauses that begin with the same conjunction, similar sentence structures, or similar or identical sentence openers. Although Fitzgerald may use three complex sentences in a row and even repeat the same type of dependent clause, he seldom seems to do so with any conscious intent other than to satisfy the necessities of what he wishes to say in those sentences. Nor does he set up any patterns within the main clauses of his sentences. Hemingway, however, not only delights in repeating words, but also sets up definite patterns within successive sentences.

Repetition of a key word can be used not only to avoid subordination, as has been illustrated, but to emphasize the importance of that word. In the following passage Hemingway uses the word or a form of the word "smoothed" three times:

> He *smoothed* out the sandy soil with his hand and pulled all the sweet fern bushes by their roots. His hands smelled good from the sweet fern. He *smoothed* the uprooted earth. He did not want anything making lumps under the blankets. When he had the ground *smooth*, he spread his three blankets.

This is not the work of a writer of limited vocabulary. Nick Adams is not only smoothing out the ground underneath him, but also smoothing out the unnecessary complications of his past, smoothing over his bruised consciousness. He wants no problems, no "lumps."

In his first description of the trout, Hemingway gives life to the stream and the fish in it by using several participial phrases to describe the scene. The trout are described as "keeping themselves steady," "holding themselves with their noses into the current," "looking to hold themselves," "facing up the current." The surface of the stream is described as "pushing and swelling." Not only are specific words repeated in these three paragraphs but the grammatical cast of those phrases used to describe the scene is identical; that is, they are all introduced by the dynamic present participle.

It has already been established that Hemingway used dependent clauses sparingly. But when he did use them he often repeated exactly the same type of clause, with the same subordinate conjunction introducing it. I have already quoted the passage describing the kingfisher in which Hemingway uses three clauses introduced by "as." Other examples abound in "Big Two-Hearted River." In the paragraph describing Nick's cogitation about the grasshoppers, five of the nine dependent clauses are introduced with "as" and three are introduced with "that." Hemingway's tendency toward repeating similar dependent clauses reduces the inherent complexity of such clauses and increases the rhythmic, ritualistic effect of his prose.

Hemingway also often repeated the structure of the larger unit of the sentence itself. In one paragraph he includes three sentences of almost identical structure:

> *He adjusted* the pack harness around the bundle, *pulling* straps tight. . . *He walked* along the road that paralleled the railway track, *leaving* the burned town behind in the heat. . . *He walked* along the road *feeling* the ache from the pull of the heavy pack.

But most striking of all is his repetition of the simple subject followed immediately by the simple verb as a sentence opener. Notice the grammatical plainness of the following passage which illustrates this type of repetition:

> *Nick sat* down beside the fire and lifted the frying pan off. *He*

poured about half the contents out into the tin plate. *It spread* slowly on the plate. *Nick knew* it was too hot. *He poured* on some tomato catchup. *He knew* the beans and spaghetti were still too hot. *He looked* at the fire, . . .

Occasionally Hemingway repeats both identical words and identical grammatical structures and, in addition, puts them in a pattern. In the following passage all of the sentences begin with the simple subject, simple verb combination and the subject is alternated:

Nick stretched under the blanket comfortably. *A mosquito hummed* close to his ear. *Nick sat* up and lit a match. *The mosquito was* on the canvas, over his head. *Nick moved* the match quickly up to it. *The mosquito made* a satisfactory hiss in the flame.

However trivial the contest, Hemingway is pitting Nick against the mosquito, just as he will later, in a more complicated sport, pit Nick against the trout. Such repetition is designed for effect. And just how effective it can become can be best illustrated in the following passage which uses all the possibilities of repetition. Nick has just set up camp, and Hemingway gives us this most unusual description of Nick's emotional state:

Now things were done. There had been this to do. Now it was done. It had been a hard trip. He was very tired. That was done. He had made his camp. He was settled. Nothing could touch him. It was a good place to camp. He was there, in the good place. He was in his home where he had made it. Now he was hungry.

Repetition of the word "done" expresses the finality of Nick's accomplishment. Repetition of the word "now," especially at the beginning of the sentences, gives the impression of shelving the past and looking with hope toward the future. All of the cobwebs have been cleared away, and he is in a "good place." All of the sentences, except one, are simple and most of the verbs express state of being rather than action. At this moment

Nick has sufficiently simplified his world, provided for all his needs, and is in a static state of simply existing. He is "settled." He is "there." Note the consistent impersonality of all of the subjects except "he:" there are "things," "this," "it," "that," "nothing." In this new world that Nick has created for himself, the "things" other than himself are without personality, without threat, unable to "touch" him. He has sufficiently neutralized his world to the point where he can satisfy his needs by repeating rituals of motion, rituals so well learned that they require no thought. The stasis of the above passage is broken only when Nick acts to satisfy his hunger.

Such manipulation of words into patterns in order to produce an effect not inherent in the lexical definition of the words themselves constitutes an attempt to escape the bounds of denotative meaning by using the rich possibilities of sentence logic to carry us beyond the words. Repetition of similar words in similar syntactical structures then adds yet another dimension of meaning. Such manipulation is not entirely outside of the province of F. Scott Fitzgerald's style. He seldom allows his sentence length or structure or word choice to become monotonous; he seldom repeats a part of a previous sentence if he can subordinate instead; there is none of the heavy-handed repetition of Hemingway in "The Rich Boy." But Fitzgerald does not altogether ignore the advantages of parallel structuring. For example, after having said: "Let me tell you about the very rich," he begins the next three sentences with: "They are," "They possess," and "They think." Here the narrator is being very straightforward and matter-of-fact. In his exquisite sentence describing the dancers upon the veranda of the Breakers in Palm Beach, Fitzgerald effectively uses repetition and syntactical structure to carry his flippancy:

> Upon the trellissed veranda of the Breakers two hundred women stepped right, stepped left, wheeled, and slid in that then celebrated calisthenic known as the double-shuffle, while in half-time to the music two thousand bracelets clicked up and down on two hundred arms.

By stringing out the active verbs "stepped," "wheeled," and "slid," Fitzgerald gives to his sentence the movement of the dance. His repetition "two hundred," "two thousand," "two hundred," intensifies the stereotyping of the dancers. But having found these devices in this sentence, we have only identified a fraction of what makes this passage so impressive. Just as much of the flippancy is carried by the single choice of words, "celebrated calisthenic," and then there is that masterful focus on the bracelets which clicked "in half-time." Repetition for effect, then, is not one of the hallmarks of Fitzgerald's style.

In fact, an examination of Fitzgerald's sentence openers reveals an unusual amount of variety. Only 54% of his sentences begin with the subject, as compared to 76% for Hemingway, and he does not fail to use all of the other possibilities at least once. The three types that he uses least often, the verbal phrase, the adjective phrase, and the front shift, all produce a certain degree of awkwardness of expression and are not at all common to our language. Sentences that begin with an adjective phrase like "Sad and depressed, he walked with his head bowed." or the front shift like "His mother he did not love," are not only awkward but difficult to grasp on first reading. Such constructions are most often found in poetry. Neither Fitzgerald nor Hemingway, in these two stories, shows any tendency to take such liberties with normal English syntax.

The last and smallest unit of written discourse, the word, is the most difficult to approach through a statistical analysis. One cannot discuss the meaning of the word but only its form, that is, the number of syllables it contains and its part of speech or function in the sentence. However, significant results can be garnered even with this limited approach. Because a study of diction necessitates identifying the part of speech of every word to be examined, this analysis of words will be limited to paragraphs four through twelve of the Fitzgerald story and paragraphs one through seventeen of the Hemingway story.

The Fitzgerald paragraphs contain 1320 words in 43 sentences; the Hemingway paragraphs contain 1446 words in 91 sentences. When considering matters of diction it is best to eliminate all function words—articles, conjunctions, and prepositions—because they are almost all monosyllabic and only add bulk to the statistics. Consequently, all figures will be based on substantive words only (nouns, verbs, verbals, adjectives, adverbs), of which the Fitzgerald story contains 930 and the Hemingway story 972.

It should come as no surprise that Hemingway's story has a larger percentage of monosyllables—72% to Fitzgerald's 61%—and a smaller percentage of words over two syllables—4% to Fitzgerald's 16%. Hemingway has long been described as having a penchant for Anglo-Saxon diction. But the difference between 61% and 72% monosyllabic words is not that spectacular, and Fitzgerald could hardly, on the basis of these statistics, be characterized as a writer who specializes in sophisticated polysyllabic diction. At the same time it is difficult to imagine Hemingway employing such phrases as "unresponsive to facetiousness," "irreproachable shadow," "verbal inhibitions," or "behavioristic demands," all of which appear in "The Rich Boy."

In addition to being considered as a measure of degree of sophistication, the number of syllables per word can be considered as a measure of degree of rhythmic flow. Whereas a succession of monosyllabic words produces a choppy effect, a succession of polysyllabic words produces a smooth, pulsating effect. Choppiness is the result of a high percentage of accents in a line. Consider the accents in the following line from "Big Two-Hearted River:"

> With the áx he slít off a bríght sláb of píne from óne of the stúmps and splít it into pégs for the tént.

Note that most of the accents fall on substantive words. Eliminate the function words and the harsh accentual effect is increased. An excellent example of this process is found in a previously quoted passage from Hemingway's story:

N ow things were done. There hád beén this to dó. Now it was
done. It hád beén a hárd trip. He 'was veŕy tired.

But this passage is exceptional, even for Hemingway. With the
normal number of function words, the difference between the
rhythm of the prose of the two writers can only be accounted
for by the number of syllables in the substantive words. The
following passage from "The Rich Boy" contains many words
of more than two syllables and hence flows easily:

> Thén, with évery opportúnity given báck to them, with nó matérial
> obstácle to overcóme, the sécret weávings of their témperaments cáme
> betwéen them, drýing up their kísses and their téars, máking their
> vóices leśs loúd to oné anóther, múffling the íntimate chátter of their
> héarts until the óld communicátion was ónly póssible by létters,
> from fár awáy.

Here, the smoothness produced by the polysyllabic diction
helps to carry the burden of the meaning of the sentence
which describes a "muffling" of passion.

It would be a mistake, however, to fail to point out that Hemingway was also capable of altering his diction to produce a
more rolling effect. His description of the rippling hills of the
jack pine country should convince us:

> . . . a lóng undulating cóuntry with fréquent ríses and descénts,
> sándy underfóot and the cóuntry alíve agáin.

Quite aside from considerations of rhythm, an author's works
are often classified as either dynamic or static on the basis of
his use of nouns and verbs. The more nouns in a passage the
more static it becomes; the more verbs, the more dynamic. The
only surprise in the percentage of substantives that are nouns
and verbs in these two stories—41% nouns or pronouns, 15%
verbs for Fitzgerald and 43% nouns or pronouns, 20% verbs
for Hemingway—is that they are so similar. Hemingway, the
man of action, writing a story filled with action, uses only 5%
more verbs than Fitzgerald and uses 2% more nouns.

63

But like any single set of statistics, the noun-verb ratio must be qualified with additional figures on the types of nouns and verbs. Linking verbs express state of being and are static. Passive verbs rob the subject, and hence the sentence, of any action. A high percentage of either engenders highly formal, dull prose. Neither Fitzgerald nor Hemingway overuses linking verbs, although the Fitzgerald story has twice as many as the Hemingway story—32% for Fitzgerald and 16% for Hemingway. Linking verbs often set up equations like "a dog is a four-legged animal," and because the Fitzgerald narrator is more argumentative and intent on close reasoning, it is natural that he should set up more equations. Both writers use an extremely high percentage of active verbs with the advantage going to Hemingway who makes 98% of his verbs active to Fitzgerald's 90%. Hemingway's lower percentage of linking verbs and higher percentage of active verbs, therefore, qualifies our earlier statements about the noun-verb ratios. A further qualification has to do with the gender of the subjects. Because the Hemingway story has only one character, the only subjects that can possess gender are those referring to Nick. All other subjects, the trout, the hills, the trees, the grasshoppers, are neuter. It would be reasonable to expect, then, that the Hemingway story contains a larger percentage of neuter subjects than the Fitzgerald story, which has many characters and is about society, and, in fact, it does contain 49% to Fitzgerald's 41%. It is much more difficult to give neuter subjects active, non-linking verbs; although grass can grow, rivers can flow, the possibilities are much more limited for action for a neuter subject. It must have taxed Hemingway's ingenuity to provide active verbs for such inanimate subjects as roads. But in one paragraph alone he provides four; the road "ran" and "reached," the country "stopped," the pine trees "rose." All of this qualifying may seem like a great deal of statistical sophistry, but it should illustrate quite well my insistence that a single statistic, isolated from other statistics and considered without relation to subject matter, is, at best, meaningless and, at worst, misleading.

Statistics will not prove, for example, that Fitzgerald is a more verbose, less economical writer than Hemingway; he employs fewer adjectives and adverbs which are commonly thought to be excess baggage for the writer who is gifted with the ability to select just the right specific noun or verb to carry all the meaning. His story has 11% adjectives to 18% for Hemingway and 7% adverbs to 12% for Hemingway. And he has less of a tendency to string together adjectives and adverbs. Yet Fitzgerald does have the reputation for being more wordy then Hemingway; and not all of it is due to Hemingway's flooding the literary periodicals with his pronouncements on cutting out unnecessary words. Once again one must look to another set of statistics and to considerations quite outside the realm of statistics to explain why Fitzgerald is accused of verbosity. Consider the differing effects on a reader of the two adjectives "gargantuan" and "big." One is a multi-syllable word that fills the mouth; the other is a simple mono-syllable. It would be conceivable, then, for two writers to use exactly the same percentage of adjectives and adverbs, and for one to give the impression of more wordiness by using multi-syllabic modifiers. As has been previously indicated, Fitzgerald does, in fact, employ more multi-syllabic words than Hemingway. Obviously the difference between "gargan-tuan" and "big" is not only a matter of length. It is also a matter of complexity. "Gargantuan" is a literary word which is seldom used in ordinary speech: "big" is a common word which is in everyone's vocabulary. A reader is instantly impressed with the complexity of a word like "gargantuan" and confuses excessive verbosity with impressive vocabulary.

The pitfalls of such impressionistic criticism of an author's style can be partially avoided by seeking the safety of numbers. But the sum of this study is by no means the whole of the styles of F. Scott Fitzgerald and Ernest Hemingway. The statistics were gathered without benefit of a computer, the use of which would have made it possible to include more pages of type in the samplings. In addition, such considerations as specificity of diction and degree of figurative language have been avoided because they require more subjective decision-making in the counting process. But even unchallengeable statistics must be correlated and interpreted. And it is when one finds it necessary to go outside of the statistics for answers that one realizes that figures alone cannot describe or explain all of what makes a writer's style uniquely his own. If this study has slighted Fitzgerald, it is because there is so much artistry in his writing that cannot be counted and turned into percentiles. Fitzgerald's forte is the striking image, the perfect detail, the effective analogy, and such devices can be measured only by critical sensitivity. A statistical analysis is useless to explain what makes the following sentence uniquely Fitz-geraldian:

> Palm Beach sprawled plump and opulent between the sparkling sapphire of Lake Worth, flawed here and there by house-boats at anchor, and the great turqoise bar of the Atlantic Ocean.

It is a simple sentence of thirty words with a subject opener. But it is much more.

Ohio State University

Texts Used:
All the Sad Young Men (New York: Scribners, 1926).
In Our Time (New York: Boni & Liveright, 1925).

APPENDIX

PROGRESSION OF HEMINGWAY'S STYLE: Data for *For Whom the Bell Tolls* comes from chapter three, paragraphs one through six. Data for *A Moveable Feast* comes from "Scott Fitzgerald," paragraphs one through three.

Description of Statistic	Big Two-Hearted River	For Whom the Bell Tolls	A Moveable Feast
Average sentence in words	12	21	24

Percentage of simple sentences	73%	28%	11%
Percentage of words inside dependent clauses	15%	32%	30%
Percentage of substantives that are monosyllables	72%	68%	70%
Percentage of substantives that are over two syllables	4%	7%	7%

PROGRESSION OF FITZGERALD'S STYLE: Data for *Tender Is the Night* comes from paragraphs one through three. Data for *The Crack Up* comes from "Early Success," paragraphs one through six.

Description of Statistic	The Rich Boy	Tender is the Night	The Crack Up
Average sentence in words	24	27	24
Percentage of simple sentences	24%	19%	21%
Percentage of words inside dependent clauses	35%	25%	32%
Percentage of substantives that are monosyllables	61%	57%	63%
Percentage of substantives that are over two syllables	16%	10%	13%

Dr. and Mrs. Roland Greene Usher
invite you to be present
at the marriage of their sister
Elizabeth Hadley Richardson
and
Mr. Ernest Miller Hemingway
on Saturday afternoon, September third
nineteen hundred and twenty-one
at four o'clock
First Presbyterian Church
Horton Bay, Michigan

R.s.v.p.
5737 Cates Avenue
Saint Louis, Missouri

Collection of C. E. Frazer Clark, Jr.

A Lost Book Review:
A Story-Teller's Story

This lost review by Ernest Hemingway of Sherwood Anderson's *A Story-Teller's Story* appeared in *Ex Libris*, II (March
1925), 176–77—the journal of the American Library in Paris—
with a companion review by Gertrude Stein. Written fourteen
months before publication of *The Torrents of Spring*—but
before he had read *Dark Laughter* (1925)—Hemingway's review
mixes warm praise for Anderson's talent with distrust of
Anderson's literary friends whose influence resulted in the
failure of *Many Marriages*. This uncertainty about Anderson's
discipline and integrity modifies the story that *Torrents* was
provoked mainly by Hemingway's desire to break his contract
with Boni & Liveright.

M. J. B.

A STORY-TELLER'S STORY, by Sherwood Anderson.
New York. B. W. Huebsch. 1924. 442 pages.

In a review of Ernest Hemingway's "In Our Time" (The Three
Mountain Press) the *Dial* recently said: "Mr. Hemingway's poems
are not particularly important, but his prose is of the first distinction. He must be counted as the only American writer but one—
Mr. Sherwood Anderson—who has felt the genius of Gertrude

Stein's 'Three Lives' and has been evidently influenced by it. Indeed Miss Stein, Mr. Anderson and Mr. Hemingway may now be said to form a school by themselves." Two of these writers have consented to give *Ex Libris* their opinion in regard to the latest book written by the third.

THE EDITOR.

The reviewers have all compared this book with the "Education of Henry Adams" and it was not hard for them to do so, for Sherwood Anderson twice refers to the Adams book and there is plenty in the "Story Teller's Story" about the cathedral at Chartres. Evidently the Education book made a deep impression on Sherwood for he quotes part of it. He also has a couple of other learned quotations in Latin and I can imagine him copying them on the typewriter verifying them carefully to get the spelling right. For Sherwood Anderson, unlike the English, does not quote you Latin in casual conversation.

As far as I know the Latin is correct although English reviewers may find flaws in it, and all of my friends own and speak of "The Education of Henry Adams" with such solemnity that I have been unable ever to read it. "A Story Teller's Story" is a good book. It is such a good book that it doesn't need to be coupled in the reviewing with Henry Adams or anybody else.

This is the Life and Times of Sherwood Anderson and a great part of it runs along in a mildly kidding way as though Sherwood were afraid people would think he took himself and his life too seriously. But there is no joking about the way he writes of horses and women and bartenders and Judge Turner and the elder Berners and the half allegorical figure of the poor devil of a magazine writer who comes in at the end of the book. And if Sherwood jokes about the base-ball player beating him up at the warehouse where he worked, you get at the same time, a very definite sharp picture of the baseball player, drunk, sullen and amazed, knocking him down as soon and as often as he got up while the two teamsters watched and wondered why this fellow named Anderson had picked a fight when he couldn't fight.

There are very beautiful places in the book, as good writing as Sherwood Anderson has done and that means considerably better than any other American writer has done. It is a great mystery and an even greater tribute to Sherwood that so many people writing today think he cannot write. They believe that he has very strange and sometimes beautiful ideas and visions and that he expresses them very clumsily and unsuccessfully. While in reality he often takes a very banal idea of things and presents it with such craftsmanship that the person reading believes it beautiful and does not see the craftsmanship at all. When he calls himself "a poor scribbler" don't believe him.

He is not a poor scribbler even though he calls himself that or worse, again and again. He is a very great writer and if he has, at times, in other books been unsuccessful, it has been for two reasons. His talent and his development of it has been toward the short story or tale and not toward that highly artificial form the novel. The second reason is that he has been what the French say of all honest politicians *mal entouré*.

In "A Story Teller's Story", which is highly successful as a piece of work because it is written in his own particular form, a series of short tales jointed up sometimes and sometimes quite disconnected, he pays homage to his New York friends who have helped him. They nearly all took something from him, and tried to give him various things in return that he needed as much as a boxer needs diamond studded teeth. And because he gave them all something he is, after the manner of all great men, very grateful to them. They called him a "phallic Chekov" and other meaningless things and watched for the sparkle of his diamond studded teeth and Sherwood got a little worried and uncertain and wrote a poor book called "Many Marriages". Then all the people who hated him because he was an American who could write and did write and had been given a prize and was starting to have some success jumped on him with loud cries that he never had written and never would be able to write and if you didn't believe it read "Many Marriages". Now Sherwood has written a fine book and they are all busy comparing him to Henry Adams.

Anyway you ought to read "A Story Teller's Story". It is a wonderful comeback after "Many Marriages".

Ernest Hemingway

A Stitch in time saves nine. Birds of a feather flock together. Chickens come home to roost.

There are four men so far in American letters who have essential intelligence. They are Fenimore Cooper, William Dean Howells, Mark Twain and Sherwood Anderson. They do not reflect life or describe life or embroider life or photograph life, they express life and to express life takes essential intelligence. Whether to express life is the most interesting thing to do or the most important thing to do I do not know, but I do know that it is the most permanent thing to do.

Sherwood Anderson has been doing this thing from his beginning. The development of the quality of this doing has been one of steady development, steady development of his mind and character, steady development in the completion of this expression. The story-teller's story is like all long books uneven but there is no uncertainty in the fullness of its quality. In detail in the beginning and it does begin, in the beginning there is the complete expression of a game, the boys are and they feel they are and they have completely been and they completely are. I think no one can hesitate before the reality of the expression of the life of the Anderson boys. And then later, the living for and by clean linen and the being of the girl who has to have and to give what is needed is without any equal in quality in anything that has been done up to this time by any one writing to-day.

The story-teller's story is not a story of events or experiences it is a story of existence, and the fact that the story teller exists makes a story and keeps on making a story. The story-teller's story will live because the story-teller is alive. As he is alive and as his gift is the complete expression of that life it will continue to live.

Gertrude Stein

The Sun Also Rises:
A Reconsideration

By

Donald T. Torchiana

Despite forty-odd years of shining existence, *The Sun Also Rises* is still read by the best of our Hemingway men as though it were an offshoot of T. S. Eliot's *Waste Land.* Sadly enough, no amount of angry denial by Hemingway himself has had much effect in removing the identification. In his latest edition of *Hemingway: The Writer as Artist,* Carlos Baker persists in entitling his chapter on the book "The Wastelanders." Though any number of statements from this chapter could be used to suggest the dogged insistence of its title, I shall pick out but one as provocative and central: "Brett . . . is . . . the reigning queen of a paganized wasteland with a wounded fisher king as her half cynical squire."[1] Perhaps even more arresting is Philip Young's stubborn assertion, coming after Hemingway's publication of *A Moveable Feast,* that "despite quite a lot of fun *The Sun Also Rises* is still Hemingway's *Waste Land,* and Jake is Hemingway's Fisher King. . . . once again here is the protagonist gone impotent, and his land gone sterile."[2] Both these critics are equally explicit in deeming the drift of the book a journey to nowhere, a study in futility, and a picture of the Lost Generation. Once again, Young is the more colorful in his attempts to talk around Hemingway's rather furious rejection of that reading:

Some support for this [Hemingway's] position can be found in the novel itself. Not quite all the people in it are "lost"—surely Romero is not—and the beauty of the eternal earth is now and then richly evoked. But most of the characters do seem a great deal of the time if not lost then terribly unsure of their bearings, and few readers have felt the force of Hemingway's intention. The strongest feeling in the book is that for the people in it (and one gets the distinct impression that other people do not matter very much) life is futile, and their motions like the motions of the sun of the title (as it appears to our eyes): endless, circular, and unavailing. Further, for all who remember what the Preacher said in this well-known Biblical passage, the echo of "Vanity of vanities; all is vanity" is rather loud. Thus what Hemingway proposed to do and what he did again seem two things, but it is doubtful that this hurts the book.[3]

If Young's is a worship of the intentional fallacy carried to the point of martyrdom, a reader may turn to Sheridan Baker's recent chapter on the book to discover a variation on that dedication that denies Hemingway's intention this time on the fact of testicles, not vanity. However Baker's previous devotions to chivalric romance may have aided him in this discovery, his outright refusal of Hemingway's blunt statement that Jake was not emasculated must be read to be believed:

Testicles and the lack of testicles—an idea Hemingway consistently associates with bullfighting, using the Spanish slang *cojones*—are clearly symbols of power and failure in *The Sun Also Rises*. . . . But whatever Hemingway's private picture of Jake's disfigurement and however that picture may have changed over the years, the similarity of Jake's deprivation to that of a steer is too insistent to be set aside.[4]

On this score—a refining on the *Waste Land* image of the novel by reducing it to a testiculate sunset—a recent critic had seemed to come to my rescue by arguing that, after all, the novel could hardly be called a study in disillusion and despair. In his essay,

"*Cabestro* and *Vaquilla*: The Symbolic Structure of *The Sun Also Rises*," Dewey Ganzel held that the bullfight rather than Eliot's poem was the proper analogy for the book. Although generally agreeing with him, I must hastily part critical company with Mr. Ganzel when he identifies Jake as a "working steer," calls Cohn, of all people, a fighting bull, and slips Brett into the role of a female fighting bull, the *vaquilla,* all of which seems to me as severely arbitrary an inversion of Hemingway's intentions as any done him by the resolute Wastelanders above.[5]

They are not without my sympathy. For, as F. Scott Fitzgerald so shrewdly observed in the year of the book's appearance, "In the mutilated man I thought Ernest bit off more than can yet be chewed between the covers of a book, then lost his nerve a little and edited the more vitalizing details out. He has since told me that something like this happened."[6] I suspect that Fitzgerald alludes to painfully sexual scenes, originally in the manuscript, revealing Jake's virility and its frustration. Accordingly, beyond removing the *Waste Land* sticker and the badge of futility from the book, I shall also turn to the bullfight, as Mr. Ganzel has done, as the analogy for the novel's structure. But I shall discover Jake, not Cohn, at the center of the book from first to last where, after the manner of a bullfighter, not a *cabestro,* he may be said to dominate the action. Thus, in trying to persuade a new generation that *The Sun Also Rises* still deserves attention on these new grounds, however shrill the objections from Fiedler, Edel, and those Hemingway used to dismiss as his New York critics, I shall open by stressing Hemingway's dislike of Eliot and his *Waste Land* point of view; then offer the alternative that the novel does indeed celebrate this enduring earth of ours, as Hemingway said it did; and finally, stretching matters a bit, take another look at the bullfight as the key to the novel's structure. So then, to the lists.

i

Hemingway's contempt for T. S. Eliot, especially during the

years immediately following publication of *The Waste Land,* is immediately apparent in the aspersions implied in the story "Mr. and Mrs. Elliot" which appeared in the *Little Review's* autumn-winter number for 1924–25. If that slander were not enough, Hemingway had also chosen to make his feelings explicit in 1924 in the October issue of the *Transatlantic Review.* The occasion was a tribute to the recently dead Joseph Conrad. One short passage is instructive:

> It is agreed by most of the people I know that Conrad is a bad writer, just as it is agreed that T. S. Eliot is a good writer. If I knew that by grinding Mr. Eliot into a fine powder and sprinkling that powder over Mr. Conrad's grave Mr. Conrad would shortly appear, looking very annoyed at the forced return, and commence writing I would leave for London early tomorrow morning with a sausage grinder.
>
> One should not be funny over the death of a great man, but you cannot couple T. S. Eliot and Joseph Conrad in a sentence seriously . . . [7]

In later years Hemingway was still able to wisecrack at Eliot's expense, although his contempt seems milder and even good-natured.[8] But with the strong hint of Mr. Elliot's impotence in the notorious story and then the even stronger hint of Mrs. Elliot's resolute Lesbianism, a reader might well expect an equal aversion in the novel. That aversion appears in fact almost at the beginning. Now it is conventional to fix upon Georgette, the little prostitute, and her remark that everyone is sick, as proof that we are indeed being ushered into another instance of the modern *Waste Land.* Yet in truth the little prostitute blithely scorns the homosexuals and affected writers that surround Braddocks—Cohn's, not Jake's, literary companion. In other words, the novel opens by introducing Robert Cohn and then moves on to record Jake's encounter with a literary set that includes Cohn and exhibits many of the traits that Hemingway had so nastily discovered in the Elliots.

Jake's pleading nausea as an excuse to rid himself of queer company is but the beginning of his, and Hemingway's, pointed revulsion against an American literary culture and life that could produce a Mencken, become absorbed in Hudson's *The Purple Land*, and, I would submit, breed a T. S. Eliot. Very little has been said of the fact that the novel from beginning to end is virtually an unrelieved attack on America. The waste land of the novel is a time and place we never see but have dinned into us with unrelieved disdain: the America of Wilson, Bryan, Ford, and Coolidge. More than once we learn that Paris is ruined by American tourists of the Woman's Club variety. Prohibition and its hypocrisy are constantly ragged. We rightly sneer at the pilgrims from Dayton, Ohio, on their way to Lourdes. The American ambassador to Spain is signalled to be the least comprehending of the entire throng watching Romero on the last day. Consequently, at the book's beginning, when locked in the midst of American writers and artists and patrons like the Braddocks, Cohn, and Frances Clyne, with attendant homosexuals in tow, we are not surprised to be introduced to Robert Prentiss, especially when told that "he was from New York by way of Chicago, and was a rising new novelist. He had some sort of an English accent." Thereafter we get the full flavor of his arch, fruity, affected conversation. Any waste land inflicted upon us is American, not Parisian.

Jake too is a writer of sorts, and Bill is a very successful one. Both have a great capacity for love of place and readily admit to being from Chicago and Kansas City. But neither cares to return to America, especially Jake. In fact, the alienated or expatriated American is held up as the true one, while we gather that the so-called good Americans at home are somehow morally at fault. As Bill quips to Jake: "You're an expatriot. You've lost touch with the soil. You get precious." The opposite is the truth. One major theme of the book emerges altogether early then, namely, Jake's love of the earth, in this case the legendary Paris of sunshine, Seine, flowering chestnut trees, and memorials to military courage. This is hardly the Anglo-American world where April is the cruellest month. Later in

The Green Hills of Africa Hemingway was to make himself explicit on the subject:

> Our people went to America because that was the place to go then. It had been a good country and we had made a bloody mess of it and I would go, now, somewhere else as we had always had the right to go somewhere else and as we had always gone. You could always come back. Let the others come to America who did not know that they had come too late. Our people had seen it at its best and fought for it when it was well worth fighting for. Now I would go somewhere else.[9]

With this heavy criticism of America, its childishness and naiveté personified in Cohn, the arrested adolescent, and his literary crowd, we are ushered into the real antidote to Eliot's *Waste Land*—the Paris of the Twenties—and its actuality, the grim fastness of distant America.

Finally, if we scrutinize Jake in his newly discovered America of the European continent, we must recognize how very unlike any Fisher King he is. In the first place, he is virile, not sterile, nor even a psychological victim, as Hemingway has been at great anatomical pains to explain. Setting off to work in Paris at the beginning of Chapter V, Jake cannot record enough of the many morning sights, smells, and sensations that delight him in his fair city, unlike Eliot's City man gloomily crossing London Bridge, coming or going to his despised bank. As the opposite of the Fisher King, Tiresias, or the generally solemn, weary, slightly deracinated and highly literary voice of *The Waste Land*, Jake, as every critic comments, has courage and friendliness a plenty with commonsense to match them. But I would go further by noting his generally good spirits and ability to laugh that rise so easily to the generally hilarious Bill and Mike. But he also harbors another quality singularly missing in Eliot's Fisher King—Jake is a fighter. As Brett explains, "You've a hell of a biblical name, Jake." He does indeed. He wrestles with life. There is nothing passive or foredoomed about him. Moreover, unlike Eliot and the Tiresias of his poem, Jake is an extremely humble man, a trait summed up in his admission to Brett that "Nobody ever knows anything." He is also a just man, forged in the disaster of the Great War, the great injustice that lies behind the book. As Hemingway once wrote, "Writers are forged in injustice as a sword is forged."[10] Like Bill, Jake is extremely sensitive to the injustice done to a Negro boxer in Vienna; he is acutely aware, as a newsman, of the difficulties of getting a true story; he won't compromise events or the telling of them, even the story of how Lady Brett came to her desperate condition. Best of all, the War has taught him impartiality—even during his jealous hatred of Cohn he admits to the man's finer qualities. Hemingway held that the great crime of war—"Never think that war, no matter how necessary, nor how justified, is not a crime"[11] —might nevertheless teach us that virtue of impartiality. As he wrote at the conclusion of World War II:

> We have come out of the time when obedience, the acceptance of discipline, intelligent courage and resolution were most important into that more difficult time when it is a man's duty to understand his world rather than simply fight for it.
>
> To understand we must study. We must study not simply what we wish to believe. That will always be skillfully presented for us. We must try to examine our world with the impartiality of a physician. This will be hard work and will involve reading much that is unpleasant to accept. But it is one of man's first duties now.[12]

Jake comes very close, in his striving to understand the new world, to that impartiality of a physician rather than to the bias of a literary doctor. His exuberant fishing, his physical maiming and psychological health, his religionless Catholicism, his love of the sun's rising rather than any implied setting, all make him very nearly a direct answer to Eliot's essentially Protestant, urban, hectoring Anglo-American Brahman.

ii

On the score of Gertrude Stein's remark, "You are all a lost generation," one may only ceaselessly repeat that Hemingway has sworn again and again that his novel was written to counter the idea of his generation's being more lost than any other. One of Hotchner's cranked-up Hemingway conversations shows his objection to be actually a commonplace, lifted as it is from several unacknowledged sources:

> That passage from Ecclesiastes, that sound lost? . . . Look, Gertrude was a complainer. So she labeled that generation with her complaint. . . . Nobody I knew at that time thought of himself as wearing the silks of the Lost Generation, or had even heard the label. We were a pretty solid mob. The characters in *Sun Also Rises* were tragic, but the real hero was the earth and you get the sense of its triumph in abiding forever.[13]

In *A Moveable Feast*, Hemingway devoted a whole chapter to mulling over Miss Stein's phrase. While admitting, with Ney's statue in mind (it also appears in the novel), that "all generations were lost by something and always had been and always would be," Hemingway's predominant sentiment in the chapter is caught in his reflection, "I thought of Miss Stein and Sherwood Anderson and egotism and mental laziness versus discipline and I thought who is calling who a lost generation?" However vicious or warmhearted Hemingway could be about Gertrude Stein, the point I wish to make here has been thoroughly overlooked. No matter how much anger Harold Loeb experienced on being the actual model for Cohn—and the vulgarity of *The Way it Was* seems to have underscored the likeness—an even closer literary resemblance would seem to be that of the fictional Cohn and Hemingway's perverse portrait of the sham Miss Stein.

Cohn, as all agree, is a pretty hopeless case. He is really a boy, at best a man formed by women who weeps easily and has nonsensical ideas about titled ladies, sportmanship, and the worth of W. H. Hudson. He doesn't drink to speak of, doesn't like Paris or fishing or bullfights, lacks breeding, is full of literary pretensions. Worst of all, he is pronouncedly a restless man, a creature who even took an inner pleasure in getting his nose flattened at Princeton, in fact, for all his bravado, a man who while sensitive to insult almost seeks it out so that he may suffer in public. In a word, he is selfish. Hemingway at the end of his life summed up his disgust with this combination of self-seeking and the hedonism that it feeds upon in these words:

> The untiring search for personal pleasure is selfishness in action. Self-exaggeration, egotism, pride, self-righteousness, self-justification and mock modesty are but branches of the tree of selfishness, whose roots run in all directions, crossing, recrossing and intertwining one another in the clay soil of personal self. Jealousy is the most insane phase of human selfishness. It is born of a selfish fear of loss or of being personally displaced by something or somebody.[14]

This appears to me to be a close résumé, abstractly speaking, of Robert Cohn, even in the matter of his frenzy over Brett's attentions to Romero, when Cohn himself admits that he must have been insane. On this concept of what might be called philosophical selfishness I would pin Cohn's resemblance to Gertrude Stein.

For it is Cohn himself who believes that his generation is liable to pass, lost to glory, and that the earth itself won't abide unless one personally seizes it. At the book's beginning Hemingway carefully distinguishes Jake and Cohn on this subject of self-concern. Jake reacts with ironic amaze at such of Cohn's plaints as "I can't stand to think my life is going so fast and I'm not really living it" or "Listen, Jake, . . . don't you ever get the feeling that all your life is going by and you're not taking advantage of it? Do you realize that you've lived nearly half the time you have to live already?" or, expectedly, "Do you know that in about thirty-five years more we'll be dead?" All these wails exemplify fear, egotism, and hedonism—but mostly fear.

Both Stein and Cohn had many fine qualities, as Hemingway repeatedly tells us. That in a sense—their being "so awful and so nice"—is why both seem such great wastes as Hemingway presents them. Both fall into an affectation of deserving merit. Neither seems to have recovered in Hemingway's eyes. At one juncture in *The Green Hills of Africa*, Gertrude Stein is condemned for having gone to pot,[15] precisely the process that Hemingway fixes on Cohn. Notoriously, the three chapters devoted to Miss Stein in *A Moveable Feast* expose her homosexuality and laziness, her hard ambition and jealousy of other writers, her lost or wasted womanhood transformed from peasant beauty to sybarite Roman emperor. The dimensions of Cohn's special perversity are far more subtle, but we sense their presence early when he rejects a bullfighter's life as an abnormal one and thus excludes himself like Gertrude Stein from life's feast. So does their itch to theorize about life and literature, an itch that clearly aligns Cohn with the male steers and makes Stein seem doubtfully feminine. Hemingway wrote in 1924: "As I have always regarded critics as the eunuchs of literature . . . But there is no use in finishing that sentence. . . . Did you, however, ever see a bull which has withstood the bad sticking of the matador, led off to the corrals by three thin steers?"[16] The answer, of course, is yes, but the point is that brave bulls and genuine writers ought to carry through, despite the critics. But Cohn and Stein did not. They lacked courage. If his fragile masculinity is redolent of the Princeton gym and the barber shop, Cohn's behavior like hers seems to be pleadingly masochistic. So much so that after levelling all about him, including for the moment Romero, Cohn is reduced to tears and bewails to Jake, of all people, his great love and the hell he has been put through. He then jumps to the rather unusual conclusion—generally settled on Jake and Hemingway—that nothing in this dreary world is of any use.

Hemingway had labeled one chapter in *A Moveable Feast* "Miss Stein Instructs." He might have just as maliciously have labeled this scene "Mr. Cohn Instructs." In one fantastic parody of his break with Miss Stein, Hemingway spoofed the whole affair by blaming it on an act of near-violence done him by her maid, who had her orders from Miss Stein.[17] Here of course

Jake's break with Cohn repeats that exaggeration as the real thing. In both cases jealousy was the motive. In any event, part of Miss Stein's going to pot Hemingway caught in the ease with which she passed out labels like "You are all a lost generation," or, in his fantasy account, "All you young men are alike." In Cohn Hemingway has made an excruciating study of just the reverse of these slogans, of a man who is a lost one and, unlike other men of his generation, ironic proof of Miss Stein's claim, even, I'm afraid, a way of directing the slur back to her and those who made her, if not her whole generation.

iii

But the tragedy of the novel is not wasted on the lost ones like Cohn and, I would imply, Stein. No, the tragedy belongs to those who truly love the earth and share in its death, though they endure in our minds for their love of it and turn the tragedy into a joyful, affectionate thing. For everywhere in *The Sun Also Rises* the earth is celebrated in her living and dying. In Paris we dote over the quintessence of its products—fine foods, vintage wines, Negro jazz, the movement of barges over the Seine, the glory of a Paris morning, the breeze that cools Jake's torments, even the courtesy of a count who has survived its savage wars. In Spain the earth's presence is even more dramatic. The fiesta itself arises traditionally and explosively from the rural ways and lives of those who flock in devotion and gaiety to it, the apex, explanation or apology for their lives. The mile after mile of dusty road, the icy trout streams, windswept plains, sudden rains and torrid suns underwrite the grapes, bulls, music and men, and assure their life in their continued destruction. This is the scene Cohn sleeps through. Neither grape nor bull nor trout stream nor dance means much to him, a nearsighted man in more than one way.

Hence, in taking this tragedy of the earth as Hemingway's acknowledged subject, as opposed to any idea of being especially lost, we may expect to be instructed in this love of an enduring though periodically dying earth. Hemingway's term is the Spanish word *aficion*, which he defined in *Death in the Afternoon* as ". . . love of bullfights. It also means the entire bull-ring public, but is usually used in the generic sense to denote the most intelligent part of the public." In the novel he simply calls it passion. To be an *aficionado*, as he goes on to explain, is to know bullfighting and for that reason to be devoted to it.

Hemingway had long held to this creed of the intelligent heart. Towards the end of his life he was explicit in saying, "The heart is the noblest part of human nature. And the affections are the noblest ingredient in human nature."[18] This saintly creed may well recall St. Firminus I, a native of Pamplona, who achieved his martyrdom in the third century and had his feast celebrated, in the manner Hemingway depicts, from the 12th century on.[19] Though the saint was noted as a missionary and preacher of the gospel in the remoter areas of heathen France, the devotions of Hemingway's celebrants are pagan. Thus, despite a good deal of speculation on the different faces offered by Jake and Brett at the church door, Hemingway's own account of the festival in 1924 certainly reinforces the religionless Catholicism or pious paganism of the event:

> There are six bull fights during the Feria and Fiesta of San Firmin. San Firmin is the local deity in the system of local idolatry which the Spaniards substitute for catholicism. San Firmin, looking very much like Buddha, is carried through the streets at odd moments during the Feria.[20]

I submit then that the passions of the heart and man's affection for other men initiated into the mysteries of the earth's diurnal round comprise the religious center of a book where *aficion* is finally attested to by the laying on of hands among the adept— one of whom is the American Jake Barnes. With the onset of seven nights and days of celebration, it is right that Jake should experience a sudden unreality, imagine himself elevated into a realm void of consequences. The cry of the natives—"Hurray for wine! hurray for the Foreigners!"—articulates his exhilaration. For he is summoned to a conviviality that aims at a brotherhood where the grape dissolves any exigencies of time and space.

For that matter, Brett's being denied entrance to the church need not underline her supposed Circe nature—that highfalutin monicker fixed on her by the literary Mr. Cohn—since no sharp division is made between the reverential darkness of the church interior and the jubilant street where Brett is garlanded and set up as an image for singing and dancing men awaiting the return of a religious procession that transports San Firmin ecstatically from church to church. In spite of her later plaint, "I'm damned bad for a religious atmosphere . . . I've got the wrong kind of face," Brett in her happiness reaffirms a faith that can include rather than exclude the supposedly narrow, doctrinal Catholicism she is said to eschew. What's more, Jake, the religious center of the book—and the center of every other theme—astounds or should astound those who smell in Brett a whiff of sacrilege. For Jake prays, as an *aficianado* should, for his friends, for the bullfighters, for himself, for money, for successful fishing and a good fiesta, and so forth. Jake finally concludes that he is not being very religious. But he truly is, for by the covenant insinuated in the book, like Brett's his passion is for the heightened life of earth worshipped with awe in both bull ring and church.

An accidental death is our reminder. If the earth has taken Jake's capacity for sexual consummation from him, so also has it taken life heedlessly from Vincente Girones. This set piece, justly celebrated for its impersonal joining of all the elements of the fiesta—from Romero's brilliant killing to Brett's impulsive affair with him—offers without comment a sacrificial victim to the earth in a rite more pagan than Christian. He had been a married farmer with two children. He had returned to the fiesta year after year until his sudden death running with the bulls. Despite the widow and children on the train bringing the coffin home, Hemingway allows us to imagine the permanence that such apparently gratuitous misery underlines: "The train started with a jerk, and then ran smoothly, going downgrade around the edge of the plateau and out into the fields of grain that blew in the wind on the plain on the way to Tafalla." So too, as I shall maintain, the tragic eventualities in the pattern of the bullfight—the supreme running with the bulls—enhance the inevitable loss that the earth demands in abiding forever. That the ear of a bull, killer of Girones, victim of Romero, should end in Jake's handkerchief jammed in a drawer with cigaret stubs is a no less symbolic affirmation of the fact that love must also end but never finish.

We must turn, then, to the bullfight to grasp the essential affirmation that I have been holding up as a non-Christian counter to the idea that the book offers only the trivial misery of a lost generation or the religious condemnation of a waste land presided over by a faithless and impotent fisher king.

iv

Hemingway makes the point both in this novel and in *Death in the Afternoon* that there is no Spanish word for bullfight. The term used—*corrida de toros*—means running with the bulls, and to run well with the bulls requires a kind of courage that finds its opposite in the antics of Robert Cohn. Hemingway himself once wrote "Courage is only another name for faith."[21] When the best bulls and men confront each other in the bull ring, the faith or confidence displayed makes the encounter a tragedy—the bull must die—yet also a rebellion against any threat of death, a sentiment Romero utters decisively in Brett's presence before his major performance: "I'm never going to die." In almost the same utterance, he boasts, "The bulls are my best friends." I take these claims to illustrate Hemingway's more explicit belief spelled out later in *Death in the Afternoon:*

> . . . rarely will a great artist with the cape and muleta be a killer. A great killer must love to kill; unless he feels it is the best thing he can do, unless he is conscious of its dignity and feels that it is its own reward, he will be incapable of the abnegation that is

necessary in real killing. The truly great killer must have a sense of honor and a sense of glory far beyond that of the ordinary bullfighter. . . . he must have a spiritual enjoyment of the moment of killing . . . One of its greatest pleasures . . . is the feeling of rebellion against death which comes from its administering. Once you accept the rule of death thou shalt not kill is an easily and a naturally obeyed commandment. But when a man is still in rebellion against death he has pleasure in taking to himself one of the Godlike attributes; that of giving it. This is one of the most profound feelings in those men who enjoy killing. These things are done in pride, and pride, of course, is a Christian sin, and a pagan virtue. But it is pride which makes the bullfight and true enjoyment of killing which makes the great matador.[22]

This rebellion against death, along with a pagan pride in killing that makes the bull's tragedy dependent on the matador's honor and the crowd's passion, demands an air of aloofness, imprinted on all of Hemingway's great bullfighters, combined with an intense local identification signaled by Montoya's disgust with Romero's gadding about with international drunks, a titled English lady, and possibly the American ambassador. Spirited human intelligence and skill pitted against pure animal courage make running with the bulls at best an ancient, traditional, indigenous, epic endeavor binding the Spanish earth into a unified landscape of animal passion, human purpose, and organic rhythm which no amount of temporary human misery can violate. This near-epic unity is glanced at openly when charged landscape after charged landscape is unfurled before us, combining, after the manner of Cezanne, an insistent geometry of land, beasts, and men in the bracing air of rural coincidence:

Looking back we could see the country spread out below. Far back the fields were squares of green and brown on the hillsides. Making the horizon were the brown mountains. They were strangely shaped. . . . Then the road came over the crest, flattened out, and went into a forest. It was a forest of cork oaks, and the sun came through the trees in patches, and there were cattle grazing back in the trees. . . . As we came to the edge of the rise

91

we saw the red roofs and white houses of Burguete ahead strung
out on the plain, and away off on the shoulder of the first dark
mountain was the gray metal-sheathed roof of the monastery of
Roncesvalles.

"There's Roncevaux," I said.

"Where?"

"Way off there where the mountain starts."

"It's cold up here," Bill said.

"It's high," I said. "It must be twelve hundred metres."

"It's awful cold," Bill said.

Here I submit is the epitome of Spanish landscape—high, cold
and near the epic site Roncevaux—a fitting memorial to the
courageous faith behind a mask of aloof coldness that recalls a
Roland, matures a Romero, and, as I shall try to argue, sits
lightly beneath the friendly exterior of Jake Barnes. This enduring earth, then, this continuous running of brave bulls and
men through centuries of Spanish soil, has about it for Hemingway the hint of holy ground, so that the peasant-centered
fiesta can be the very antidote to Eliot's prescriptive verses
condemning an unreal City, London's financial district, the
capital of world usury. Nor can St. Mary Woolnoth's, the
banker's church, offer the refuge of the Spanish countryside or
the certainties and sparkle of Hemingway's springtime in Paris.
The earth becomes the hero, as Hemingway claimed. Eliot's
City languishes for just such holiness, unaided even by memories of Essex, Magnus Martyr, and Conrad's Marlow.

His own love of countryside and people has long been an
open secret in Hemingway lore. We are not surprised to find
him writing explicitly, "I have loved country all my life; the
country was always better than the people. I could only care
about a very few at a time."[23] Like the heady delicacy of Paris,
the Spanish earth—more tragic, less self-conscious—joins in
Hemingway's nostalgic celebration of an all but vanished America. Bill and Jake can still marvel at the fiesta as it dramatizes
totally the life and death of significant country. Packed with
peasants in black, the "solid and unbroken fiesta" absorbs all

who approach it. Even on the last day, distraught Americans, gaping English, Mike's creditors, government officials, the wanderers of all nations are caught up in its saturnalia with the vaunted tragedy of the bull ring and the martyrdom of St. Firminus at its center. This is the stuff for the American writer who has chosen not to return home, the density of felt life that those critics who carp about expatriot removal from reality—"you're not in touch with the soil"—have missed in *The Sun Also Rises.* Writing of Elio Vittorini's experience of Italy, Hemingway in 1949 contrasted such a writer's evocation of Sicily through its rainfall with those New York critics' abstract grasp of America or Italy, and, in angrily forcing the contrasts, clarifies his American love of the myriad Spanish earth:

> ... Vittorini from the time he was old enough to leave home without permission at seventeen learned his native Italy in the same way American boys who ran away from home learned their own country.

> The Italy that he learned and the America that the American boys learned has little to do with the Academic Italy or America that periodically attacks all writing like a dust storm and is always, until everything shall be completely dry, dispersed by rain.

> Rain to an academician is probably, after the first fall has cleared the air, H_2O with, of course, traces of other things. To a good writer, needing something to bring the dry country alive so that it will not be a desert where only such cactus as New York literary reviews grow dry and sad, inexistent without the watering of their benefactors, feeding on the dried manure of schism and the dusty taste of disputed dialectics, their only flowering a desiccated criticism as alive as stuffed birds, and their steady mulch the dehydrated cuds of fellow critics; such a writer finds rain to be made of knowledge, experience, wine, bread, salt, vinegar, bed, early mornings, nights, days, the sea, men, women, dogs, beloved motor cars, bicycles, hills and valleys, the appearance and disappearance of trains on straight and curved tracks, love, honor and disobey, music, chamber music and chamber pots, negative and positive Wassermanns, the arrival and non-arrival of expected

munitions and/or reinforcements, replacements or your brother. All these are part of rain to a good writer . . .

In this book the rain you get is Sicily.[24]

The Spanish earth, like the rain in Sicily, was to become during the Spanish Civil War proof positive that the American dead of the Lincoln Battalion would be immortal. Hemingway's later pronouncement on their continued life echoes the passage above on the mystical substance of rain. It also highlights his devotions to Spanish countryside and its yearly fiesta, his announced master theme of the novel: human tragedy on an earth that endures forever:

> The dead sleep cold in Spain tonight and they will sleep cold all this winter as the earth sleeps with them. But in the spring the rain will come to make the earth kind again. The wind will blow soft over the hills from the south. The black trees will come to life with small green leaves, and there will be blossoms on the apple trees along the Jarama River. This spring the dead will feel the earth beginning to live again.
>
> For our dead are a part of the earth of Spain now and the earth of Spain can never die. Each winter it will seem to die and each spring it will come alive again. Our dead will live with it forever.
>
> Just as the earth can never die, neither will those who have ever been free return to slavery. The peasants who work the earth where our dead lie know what these dead died for. There was time during the war for them to learn these things, and there is forever for them to remember them in.
>
> Our dead live in the hearts and minds of the Spanish peasants, of the Spanish workers, of all the good, simple, honest people who believed in and fought for the Spanish republic. And as long as all our dead live in the Spanish earth, and they will live as long as the earth lives, no system of tyranny ever will prevail in Spain.
>
> The fascists may spread over the land, blasting their way with weight of metal brought from other countries. They may advance aided by traitors and by cowards. They may destroy cities and

villages and try to hold the people in slavery. But you cannot hold any people in slavery.

The Spanish people will rise again as they have always risen before against tyranny.

The dead do not need to rise. They are a part of the earth now and the earth can never be conquered. For the earth endureth forever. It will outlive all systems of tyranny.

Those who have entered it honorably, and no men ever entered earth more honorably than those who died in Spain, already have achieved immortality.[25]

As a matter of fact, Hemingway came to see those American dead in Spain as joined with those others who fought in our own Civil War.[26]

Thus the tragedy of the bull ring, stemming from the strength and virtues of the Spanish landscape, concentrates the tragedy of Jake and his friends, a tragedy comprehensible to the initiated, whether from Italy, America, Africa or wherever—wherever being those specific locales ranged over the world that Hemingway loved and, metaphorically, claimed as his lost America. Jake Barnes takes his place in a pantheon of American heroes, that includes Robert Jordan, a precisionist from even farther west than Kansas City, who act out Hemingway's rediscovery of his native land. Like those later veterans of Spain, Jake does his duty like the airman he once was. The same may be said on a more mystical level of Romero, if one keeps in mind the demands of the traditional bullfight audience. In neither case does death in the ring or in bed prevail. For in *The Sun Also Rises*, America and Spain, Jake and Romero, join hands on the Spanish earth to outlast that threat. Hemingway seldom made the point more clearly—tragedy's exultation over death, the daily drama of Jake and Romero—than when he wrote:

It was a saying of Milton that, "Who best can suffer, best can do." The work of many of the greatest men, inspired by duty, has been done amidst suffering and trial and difficulty. They have struggled against the tide and reached the shore exhausted, only to grasp the sand and expire. They have done their duty and been content to die. But death has no power over such men; their hallowed memories still survive to soothe us.[27]

v

What is the structure of this tragedy—or perhaps I should say this life of earth or bull ring with its tragedy always imbedded and awaiting us? If it cannot be the circular, futile thing, that critics lead us to believe, and if the tragedy itself is a much more joyous, pagan thing than any Christian lament over the lacrimae rerum might allow, then the bull ring must be the test of any new theory of structure. Since it lies at the center of the book, I shall argue that its drama is the drama of the novel.

According to Hemingway, bullfighting demonstrates man's dominance over animals, the bull being one of the most formidable. Hemingway goes so far as to picture the final third of the contest, the faena, in terms of religious and tragic ecstasy:

> . . . the faena that takes a man out of himself and makes him feel immortal while it is proceeding, that gives him an ecstasy that is, while momentary, as profound as any religious ecstasy; moving all the people in the ring together and increasing in emotional intensity as it proceeds, carrying the bullfighter with it, he playing on the crowd through the bull and being moved as it responds in a growing ecstasy of ordered, formal, passionate, increasing disregard for death that leaves you, when it is over, and the death administered to the animal that has made it possible, as empty, as changed and as sad as any major emotion will leave you.[28]

Such emotion, I hope to show, lies close to the feeling Hemingway rouses at the end of *The Sun Also Rises*. It is not a feeling of futility, for all its sadness. Alive, Jake is increasingly superior in the last portion of the novel to the death of his own sexual power. Overwhelmed increasingly by the animalism all around him, he nevertheless prevails and dominates as a man. Let us contemplate his persistent domination of the book.

96

Jake is no bullfighter. He kills no one. Nor had Hemingway written *Death in the Afternoon*, the source of my recent quotations, until some years after this novel. Nevertheless, in October 1923, he published news stories in the *Toronto Star* on both bullfighting and Pamplona, obvious sources for his fiction as was so much of his journalism during those years. Dwelling upon the ancient, pagan, and tragic origins of the spectacle in both articles, he offers to explain in the first the structure of the fight. He insists that it is not to be confused with sport. Instead, "It is a tragedy. A very great tragedy. The tragedy is the death of the bull. It is played in three definite acts." Hemingway goes on to explain each of the acts, all together a tragedy that "symbolizes the struggle between man and beasts" where vulgarity is the worst sin a bullfighter can commit. In the first the bull arrives promptly met by picadors defending their mounts with lances. The horses are gone in the second act; the matador places the banderillas which, if correctly planted, further confuse the bull and slow him down. The third act promises the death of the bull, the chore of the matador, who has actually been in command since the opening of hostilities in the first act. His killing must be perfect. With the time and place of the sword thrust rigidly prescribed, the matador must constantly dominate the bull by close work with the muleta right down to the killing. Summing up matters in this first article, Hemingway wrote of the matador: "He must be proficient in all three acts of the fight. In the first he uses the cape and does veronicas and protects the picadors by taking the bull out and away from them when they are spilled to the ground. In the second act he plants the banderillos. In the third act he masters the bull with the muleta and kills him."[29] As Hemingway was to elaborate in *Death in the Afternoon*, all the bull's likely victories occur in the first act, considered the trial. Thereafter he faces sentencing in the second act and execution in the third. The drift is both preordained and nonAnglo-Saxon. The great requirements are bright sunshine and a windless day, hardly the concomitants, say, of *Lear*, *Hamlet*, or for that matter *The Waste Land*.

I shall not claim, as has Dewey Ganzel, that Cohn must be considered the bull if this scheme is to fit the novel—although he is stupidly dangerous when, like the bulls in Pamplona, we find him isolated from his companions. Nor, if you choose to cast Cohn in the role of the fighting bull, could he be said to make much of a fight of the book. Unlike the ideal, vicious, fearless, fighting bull, Cohn has little breeding, less bravery, and no proximity to the wolf, Hemingway's analogue for such a bull. Nevertheless, Jake has a formidable enough opponent, which he dominates like a good matador at the risk of his manhood and without inflicting needless pain.

I speak of the totally bad form, to one degree or another the poor faith, in the long run the collective animality—attractive, vicious, magnificent, and irrational—exhibited by Jake's friends. The bull is, so to speak, the undeterred compulsions of those friends. Their tragedy is imaginatively like that of the bull—an irrational, determined, even deliberate charge into dissolution maddened by the impetus of the War. By contrast, Hemingway insists in Jake that the ultimate dissolution of bull, man or earth must be met with style, cheerfulness, control, and even artistically bestowed indifference. Playing this role as close to his companions as love will allow, Jake's countering them gives their tragedy significance.

How then does this tripartite structure of the bullfight match up imaginatively with the three sections of the novel? Though the likeness isn't perfectly exact, the parallels exist in a rough but startling way. Just as the bullfight is a series of downhill actions for the bull, with the matador hopefully looking better and better—Hemingway saw the bull moving through three stages, lofty, slowed, and leaden—so during the three sections of the book Jake's friends are brought to a virtual standstill. Cohn, Brett, Mike, even to some extent Bill, isolated in their baffled desires become more and more dangerous because at the same time more and more ashamed, abandoned, busted or exhausted until they are brought around, humanized or politely dismissed by the quietly resolute Jake. Thus in the first book, and perhaps beyond to include the arrival of Bill and Mike before the departure for Spain, animalism seems to triumph on all sides. Even Robert Cohn finds himself a success at cards, a published novelist of a bad book, and very much the possessive and deserving swain of a titled lady, who at the end has agreed to go off with him to San Sebastian. Brett, though in love with Jake and miserable for keeping this tryst from him—the refrain of the last song they dance to is "Don't Two Time Me"—quite successfully inflicts her unintentional cruelties on him. She stands Jake up, bedazzles the Count, runs off with Cohn, and returns with Mike in tow. Nor is Mike as gentle or thoughtful as we might have expected, harping drunkenly before Jake on Brett's sexual attractiveness. Even Bill, befuddled as he is when we first meet him at the beginning of Book II, holds forth on the subject with more than enough insistence. Minor figures, too, like Frances Clyne, Harvey Stone, the Braddockses, and the American tourists give Jake sore moments. However, although a few horses are nicked, like Jake's concierge the first time she meets Brett, and the patronne's daughter after her run-in with Georgette, Jake manages to keep his entourage off each other and himself by a combination of skillful dodges, compassionate understanding, as with Brett and Harvey Stone, and iron determination to get on with his own work. In fact, for all their confused verve and mad comings and goings, Jake quietly dominates them by seeming not to. He has even made out the itinerary for Spain, when all in good humor leap off for the fiesta, knowing they will be in touch with each other, thanks to Jake's painstaking.

The explosion of the fiesta at Pamplona corresponds to the increased confusion of all but Jake, although he is harried enough. As the matador brings out the best in a bull by placing the banderillas right, so Jake attempts to bring out the best in his friends—what more conducive to deepfelt friendship than a fiesta?—yet each act of friendship also goads the jealousy, the disgust, the false heroics, the sluttishness in, respectively, Mike,

Bill, Cohn, and Brett. Jake *intends* nothing of the sort. But in keeping with my analogy, a reader senses that Jake quickly faces the inevitable, the compulsive nature of their behavior and so in humoring them along unaffectedly draws them out, even tires them and himself in fighting his delaying action—Roncevaux again—where only he and perhaps Bill hold on. In one famous passage, Bill inadvertently hints that Jake's role is that of the unfortunate friend-making steers. In another Mike accuses Cohn of being a steer—hanging around when he's not wanted. But Jake is no steer, and Cohn's unmanly dependence is but the worst part of a collective animality that knocks Jake off his feet. Old Jake, the human punching bag, as Bill dubs him, nevertheless gets on his feet again and is left standing with Cohn run off to Paris in shame, Brett in bed with Romero, and Mike in general disgrace. Jake himself has been called a pimp, is out of favor with Montoya, and has been knocked silly. Such are the rewards for enlivening the existence of his friends—the bulls. We are ready for the last act, the faena.

In the third book, out of Pamplona, Jake does more than hold on. Although Mike is left to live on credit and Bill drifts off, the challenge of animality however weakened remains dangerous and unpredictable in Brett's call for help. Quelling now the beast in himself, Jake gallantly returns to Spain. Like the matador at one with the bull at the moment of the kill, he seeks Brett out and brings her away. At the close of the novel he may well retort to her thought at what might have been, "Isn't it pretty to think so," but at this expected halt in traffic we not only realize that their life can be no different, we are also persuaded that the traffic will move on, that Jake will come to Brett's rescue again, and that their meeting then, as at the book's beginning, will be repeated. So the earth turns, the earth Jake loves, the earth that breeds such people and such bulls—vicious, simple, hostile, grand—but Jake has braved them and will brave and love again. He brings out the best in his friends, if we consider the entire course of his running with them, while Cohn the boxer brought out the worst.

These considerations lead me to a no less audacious conclusion. Namely that *The Sun Also Rises* is a novel of sculptured masses, the phrase and configuration which delighted Hemingway in the bull ring, here seen in a series of mounting dangers which Jake faces without flinching, gifted, as he is, as an American who believes that death is a friend, since it is the only thing a man may be certain of.[30] Like the bullfighters he praises at the book's beginning, he too lives his life up to the hilt. The French and the English, who do not always show up well in the novel, contrast with Jake. They, the life-lovers, the animal-lovers, the gold-sniffers, the real fantastics at Pamplona, lack Jake's keen thought, yes, intellectual respectability, grounded as his actions are on the certainty of death. To write of Hemingway that ". . . nowhere in Hemingway's work does there glimmer even the faintest suggestion that one's life can be ordered by thought, or that it is at all desirable to attempt such an offering. . . . the Hemingway hero lacks the intellectual resources to achieve a distance from his suffering, to contemplate it, and to learn something from it fundamental about himself"[31] —to write thus, or to parrot Yeats and claim that "Jake lacks much conviction,"[32] is tacitly to conceive of the novel as at best an understated, ironic, purgatorial rendition of *The Waste Land*. Little more than bumbtious humor, a stiff upper lip, the code hero of the Twenties, or an anatomy of society patently lifted from *Huckleberry Finn* can be the stale rewards for such a reading. On the other hand, to remember Hemingway's remark that Descartes was unduly sanguine "when he wrote in the seventeenth century, 'Good sense is, of all things among men, the most equally distributed' "[33] or that "the world of a man's life is, for the most part, the world of his thoughts"[34] may help fix the dimensions of Jake Barnes that I have been urging: a man of commonsense indeed but also a man whose devotion to the bull ring has taught him the value of courageous rationality, a trait he exhibits with increasing intensity as he moves through his turbulent heavens—fishing, reading,

101

writing, cheerful and friendly concern for his fellows—in a pre-ordained dying world. His thoughts, doubts, judgments and intellection triumph over the equally precious animalism that has been his tormentor, main spring and personal tragedy. As with Romero in the ring, Jake's manner and thought are one since the earth does endure forever.

Northwestern University

---

[1] *Hemingway: The Artist as Writer* (Princeton: Princeton University Press, 1963), 3rd ed., p. 90.

[2] *Ernest Hemingway: A Reconsideration* (University Park: Pennsylvania State University Press, 1966), pp. 87–88.

[3] *Ibid.*, p. 87n.

[4] *Ernest Hemingway: An Introduction and Interpretation* (New York: Holt, Rinehart & Winston, 1967), pp. 50–51. For Hemingway's statement that Jake's "testicles were intact and not damaged," see George Plimpton's interview in *Writers at Work, Second Series* (New York: Viking, 1965), p. 230.

[5] *"Cabestro* and *Vaquilla*: The Symbolic Structure of *The Sun Also Rises,"* *Sewanee Review,* LXXVI (Winter 1968), 26–48.

[6] *The Letters of F. Scott Fitzgerald,* ed. Andrew Turnbull (New York: Scribners, 1963), p. 205.

[7] "Conrad, Optimist and Moralist," *By-Line: Ernest Hemingway,* ed. William White (New York: Scribners, 1967), pp. 132–33.

[8] See for instance *Death in the Afternoon,* pp. 139–40, and *A Moveable Feast,* pp. 110–13.

[9] *The Green Hills of Africa,* p. 285.

[10] *Ibid.,* p. 71.

[11] "Foreword," *Treasury for the Free World,* ed. Ben Raeburn (New York: Arco, 1946), p. xv.

[12] *Ibid.,* p. xiii.

[13] *Papa Hemingway* (New York: Random House, 1966), pp. 49–50.

[14] "Advice to a Young Man," *Playboy,* XI (January 1964), 227.

[15] *The Green Hills of Africa,* pp. 65–66.

[16] "New York," *Transatlantic Review,* I (May 1924), 355.

[17] "My Own Life," *The New Yorker Scrapbook* (Garden City, N.Y.: Doubleday, Doran, 1931), pp. 156–57.

[18] *Playboy,* 225.

[19] Rev. Alban Butler, *The Lives of the Saints,* rev. by Herbert Thurston and Donald Attwater, IX (London, 1934), p. 310.

[20] "Pamplona Letter," *Transatlantic Review,* II (September 1924), 301.

[21] *Playboy,* 225.

[22] *Death in the Afternoon*, pp. 232–33.

[23] *The Green Hills of Africa*, p. 66.

[24] "Introduction" to Elio Vittorini, *In Sicily* (New York: New Directions, 1949), n.p.

[25] "On the American Dead in Spain," *Somebody Had to Do Something: A Memorial to James Phillips Lardner* (Los Angeles, 1939), pp. 4–5.

[26] "The Last Commander and Unpublished Letters," *American Dialog*, I (October-November 1964), 10.

[27] *Playboy*, 227.

[28] *Death in the Afternoon*, pp. 206–07.

[29] "Bull Fighting a Tragedy," *By-Line: Ernest Hemingway*, pp. 97–98.

[30] *Death in the Afternoon*, p. 66.

[31] Robert Evans, "Hemingway and the Pale Cast of Thought," *American Literature*, XXXVIII (1966), 168.

[32] David Fuchs, "Ernest Hemingway, Literary Critic," *American Literature*, XXXVI (1965), 447.

[33] Mary Hemingway, "Life with Papa," *Flair*, II (January 1951), 116.

[34] *Playboy*, 226.

Hemingway At Auction:
A Brief Survey

By

C. E. Frazer Clark, Jr.

Three Stories & Ten Poems[1] and *in our time*[2] have been selected as the basis for this survey of Hemingway at auction for the important reasons that no serious collection of Hemingway's work can be built without copies of both titles, and the record of their auction prices patterns the changing taste and determination of private and institutional buyers alike. Additionally, both titles are sufficiently scarce to insure attention whenever they appear under the hammer.

Charted out, the prices realized by *3 & 10* and *iot* reflect a markedly similar pattern and, in accumulation, expose the aggressively accelerated changes in the rare book market. Prices pegged by the two titles track a remarkably stable pattern from 1930 through the mid-fifties, with some hardening on bargain knock-downs as the market soaks up the first spate of both titles. More than thirty offerings appear from 1930 through 1942, combined titles and reappearing copies. Less than half this number come up during the period 1943–1957. Finally, beginning in the late fifties and continuing a spiral upward with yet undiminished vigor, the Hemingway auction record dramatically reflects the pressures which have boomed the rare book market—growing collector conviction, aggressive new institutional acquisitions campaigns, and inflation hedge buying.

Hemingway first appears in American auction records with the sale, March 10, 1930, at The Ritter-Hopson Galleries in New York, of a fine copy of *iot*. The price paid was a stiff $160—$10 more than was paid the same year for Nathaniel Hawthorne's holograph copy-book containing an unpublished manuscript poem. Appropriately, the purchaser of the Ritter-Hopson *iot* was Hemingway's first bibliographer, the great bookman, Captain Louis Henry Cohn, whose efforts did much to establish and promote Hemingway as a collected author.[3] Two months after the Ritter-Hopson sale, the first Hemingway item to reach auction in England, also a copy of *iot*, was knocked down at Puttick & Simpson, London, May 8, 1930, for £ 11/10.[4]

On January 23, 1931, at The American Art Association Anderson Galleries, the first copy to appear at auction of Hemingway's first book, *3 & 10*, was sold for $85. A second copy the same year brought $78, and copies the following year fetched $45 and $130. *3 & 10* did not appear at auction in England until March 4, 1936, at Hodgson & Co., where it brought £ 7/15.

The first joint appearance at auction of *3 & 10* and *iot* came October 27-28, 1931, at the Chicago Book and Art Auction, with *iot* bringing $88 and *3 & 10* $78. This same proportionate differential in the price of the two Hemingway rarities has generally held true through the entire history of Hemingway at auction (and in dealer catalogues). The edge in auction pricing in favor of *iot* reflects the greater scarcity of *iot* based on a reported printing of 170 copies versus 300 copies of *3 & 10*.[5]

The $160 Captain Cohn paid for the first Hemingway item at auction effectively pegged the price for Hemingway rarities for the first 27 of the 38 successive years of accumulated Hemingway auction history. Only four times during the period 1930 through 1957 was $160 topped, and each time it took a matched pair to do it. The first time was at the American Art Association Sale, January 29-30, 1936, when a pace-setting pair of *3 & 10* and *iot* were hammered down at a record of $230 and $190 respectively. At the Frank Hogan Sale, January 23-24, 1945, another pair, inscribed to Hogan, was sold for $200 and $170 respectively. With these exceptions, *every* other Hemingway item—book, manuscript, letter—appearing at auction between 1930 and 1957 could be had for $160 or less—including a number of fine presentation or association items.

An interesting problem that might be extrapolated from the auction record and general stability of Hemingway prices from 1930 through 1957 is the extent to which the popularity of an author's work or the publicity surrounding a colorful life can influence the collecting of his work. Consider—no Hemingway item—book, manuscript, or letter—appears at auction until his literary reputation has been unalterably established through the publication of his first seven books, including a hugely successful printing of something over 80,000 copies of *A Farewell to Arms* in its first six months, a Hollywood production, and personal publicity of immense proportions. In addition, in a twenty-seven-year period following his first appearance at auction, no single Hemingway item—book, manuscript, or letter—brings much more than the $160 Captain Cohn first paid—even though all the major works of Hemingway's fantastically successful and productive career come before the public. In spite of the monumental sales of *For Whom the Bell Tolls*, the capping success and acclaim for *The Old Man and The Sea*, and the Award of the Pulitzer Prize, announced May 4, 1953, it was still possible to buy a copy of *3 & 10* for $120.

The highest price paid for *any* Hemingway item at auction from 1930 through 1957 is the $230 recorded in 1936 for the copy of *3 & 10* inscribed to Sylvia Beach. For the same period, the greatest total price for Hemingway lots offered at one sale was achieved in the E. W. Titus Sale, October 8-9, 1951, when seven lots, including the manuscript of Hemingway's article "Homage to Ezra," the typescript of the Introduction to *Kiki's*

Memoirs, heavily corrected, together with the corrected page proofs, the typescript of his story "The Sea Change," several letters, and copies of both *3 & 10* and *iot*, brought something just under $800.

Only seven years later, on October 14, 1958, the library of Dr. Don Carlos Guffey was offered at Parke-Bernet Galleries in New York, and Hemingway collectors had their first crack at a major Hemingway Collection. Dr. Guffey "was fortunate enough to be chosen by Mr. Hemingway as the obstetrician for Pauline when she had her children. Mr. Hemingway was then writing *Farewell to Arms.* He inscribed at length many of the volumes of this collection, and was generous as their perusal will clearly prove."[6] The forty-one Hemingway lots in the Guffey Sale brought a record total of $19,805. Of this total, $13,000 (plus 10% commission) was paid by The University of Texas for the working manuscript (311 pages) of the major portion of *Death in the Afternoon.* This was the only major Hemingway manuscript to come up at auction, and it set a record for the greatest price paid for an American literary manuscript auctioned during the author's lifetime.

The Guffey copies of *iot* and *3 & 10*, both inscribed to Guffey, brought record prices of $900 and $750 respectively. The *iot* carried a full page recollection by Hemingway of the history surrounding the publication of this title—bibliographical significance which would help justify a steep bid. The *3 & 10* bore only a brief personal presentation note to Dr. Guffey, yet this title also earned a record bid.

In all respects, the Guffey Sale's Hemingway total of $19,805 was spectacular and demonstrated a dramatic change in the auction market's attitude toward Hemingway material, particularly good material. This bullish charge, with occasional adjustments, continued through the Chord, Weinberg, and Hamilton Sales[7] of substantial Hemingway offerings and reached its current zenith in the spectacular record of $2800 happily battled out by a number of bold competitors for the *iot* inscribed to Sylvia Beach—the same copy which fetched a healthy $190 in 1936, but brought only $150 12 years later in the March 1, 1948, Wallack Sale.[8]

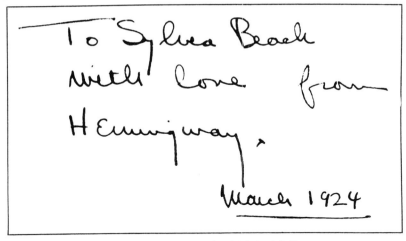

To Sylvia Beach
with Love from
H Emingway.

March 1924

$190 in 1936 — $2,800 in 1968.

There is no simple explanation for the auction performance at the Guffey Sale—equally, any explanation which suggests Hemingway had now sufficiently seasoned to warrant greater attention, or that this is just a general reflection of the overall rare book boom, or a fact of inflation, or a recognition of new institutional money in the market risks oversimplification—it's too easy an answer. In the case of Hemingway, there are specific factors at work which need to be considered. When Texas spent $13,000 for the manuscript of *Death in the Afternoon*, it might be said that Texas had ample discretionary funds and, after all, it was Texas. Still—Texas had to decide it wanted this particular material and that it was sufficiently important material to pay an unheard-of price—and that it had to beat out at least one spirited underbidder with almost as much conviction.

A number of things happened between the time of the Titus Sale (October, 1951), the last sale before the Guffey Sale at which an important offering of Hemingway material was made, and the record-setting Guffey Sale in October, 1958. In September, 1952, *The Old Man and The Sea* was published and while it didn't smoke out any great caches of Hemingway for auction, it did do much to restore high critical acclaim for Hemingway's literary artistry. *Old Man* also undoubtedly contributed substantially to the decisions to award Hemingway the Pulitzer Prize (1952) and the Nobel Prize (1954), both of which materially confirmed his position as the ranking man of American Letters.

Perhaps even more significant was the appearance in 1952 of three major critical works on Hemingway—*Hemingway: The Writer as Artist,* by Carlos Baker; *Ernest Hemingway,* by Philip Young; and *The Art of Ernest Hemingway,* by John Atkins. Baker includes in his book "A Working Check-List of Hemingway's Prose, Poetry, and Journalism—with Notes," which proved to be the best working bibliography of Hemingway's work produced to date, which contributed sufficiently to a demand for the title to insure an enlarged second edition by 1956. A fourth major critical study previewed in 1952 when sections of Charles A. Fenton's *The Apprenticeship of Ernest Hemingway: The Early Years,* appeared in periodical form. The book appeared in 1954 and insured its author a place as participant in the National Broadcasting Company's hour-long documentary "Meet Ernest Hemingway." These four major works on Hemingway opened the door on a determined era of Hemingway scholarship, which has continued unabated. Baker, Young, Atkins, and Fenton established that Hemingway was a subject to be studied, and studied full-bore.

Now, in all the institutions where Hemingway scholars picked up the track, resource materials had to be found, the raw material of scholarship, books, manuscripts, letters, had to be acquired. Now, acquisition programs for a build-up of significant Hemingway Collections were formed and Acquisition Staffs began beating a hot path to dealers and the auction floor. What made the hunt all the more attractive was that Hemingway, un-like Hawthorne and the other established figures, was not all collected out, and the hoardes with their long-ago firmly staked-out claims did not yet exist. A further incentive was that Hem-ingway was both available and dirt cheap compared with the market on the other greats collected. Hemingway was a bargain in the mid-fifties by any standard and, in retrospect, an obvious and incredible bargain any time after the war years. The appre-ciation in value of collections built at that time is almost un-believable.

What Baker, Young, Atkins, and Fenton really proved, how-ever, is that scholarship sells rare books.

By the time of the Guffey Sale, the boom in rare books was on; some of the inflationary pressures were beginning to be felt; Hemingway had reached the height of his career; the market had been dry for a while; and the quality of the material offered was exceptional. All this contributed to the record prices real-ized—but the fact remains that repositories of scholarship and scholar-inspired collectors took home most of the bacon. Schol-arship has a direct and determinable effect on the rare book auction market, if the record of Hemingway at auction in 1958 or since is to be weighed.

Show-stopper copies of both *iot* and *3 & 10* have been reg-ularly available throughout the auction history of Hemingway material, with certain copies appearing more than once. The most famous, the inscribed pair to Sylvia Beach, have come up three times (1936 - $190; 1948 - $150; 1968 - $2800; for *iot.* 1936 - $230; 1948 - $150; 1968 - $1900; for *3 & 10*). In each case they were offered together and kept together until the Feinberg Sale in 1968 when they were purchased by separate buyers.

Another important reappearing copy is the *3 & 10* inscribed by Hemingway to James Richardson, brother of Hemingway's

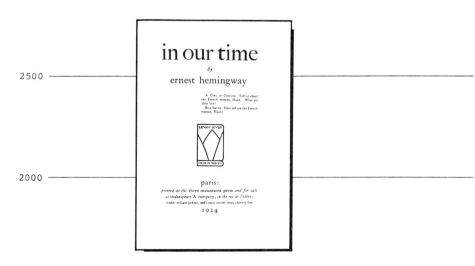

3000 —

2500 —

2000 —

1500 —

AUCTION
RECORD

1000 —

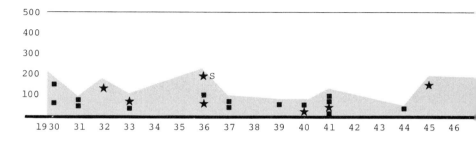

500 —
400
300
200
100

1930   31   32   33   34   35   36   37   38   39   40   41   42   43   44   45   46

★ - Signed, Presentation, or Association Copy

S - Copy inscribed to Sylvia Beach

R - Copy inscribed to James Richardson

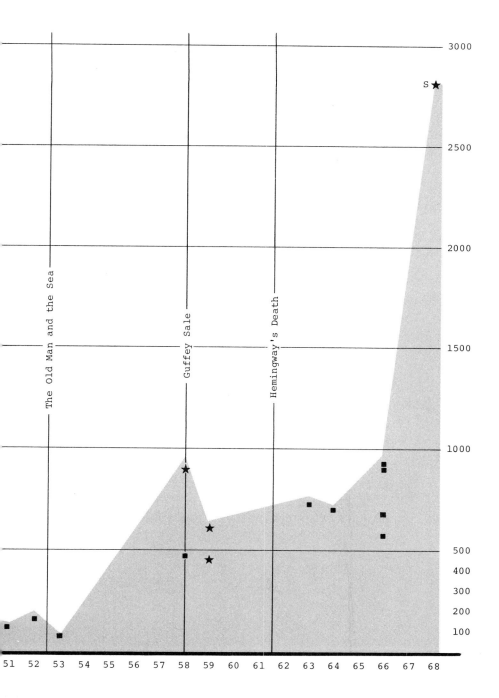

first wife, Hadley (to whom the book is dedicated). This, together with a copy of *iot* also inscribed to James Richardson, first appears at the Frank Capra Sale at Parke-Bernet, April 26, 1949. At the sale, *iot* brings $160, and *3 & 10* a modest $120. Now minus its companion, the Richardson *3 & 10* next appears in the Chord Sale, April 9–10, 1963, where it brings $675. May 24, 1966, the Richardson copy makes its last appearance to date bringing a record $1900—the same price fetched for the Beach *3 & 10* two years later.

The Guffey copies of *3 & 10* and *iot* deserve special mention in that a careful scrutiny of the sale catalogues reveals that there were actually three matched pairs of these titles, all inscribed to Dr. Guffey. The first pair were the record-setting duo which brought $750 for *3 & 10* and $900 for *iot* in the landmark 1958 Guffey Sale. Only six months later, 28–29 April 1959, a second pair also inscribed to Dr. Guffey are offered. This on-the-heels appearance takes something of the edge off the market and the second inscribed Guffey *3 & 10* brings only $400 while the second inscribed Guffey *iot,* with an 11 line inscription concerning the frontispiece for *iot,* brings $600. A short eight months later at the Whitman Bennet Sale, 8 December 1959, a third Guffey pair, both inscribed, turn up. Both titles fetch an understandably hesitant $450, even though Dr. Guffey's third *3 & 10* has been improved with a 23 line inscription plus a 5 line insertion concerning McAlmon and The Contact Publishing Co. An appreciation of Dr. Guffey's enthusiastic collecting might be found in Hemingway's inscription in the copy of *3 & 10* offered 28–29 April 1959—"To Dr. Don Carlos Guffey. This book purchased at great expense by him hoping if he is to read he will not wait for the market to reach top."

These and other inscribed copies of both titles have appeared often enough in the collecting lifetime of many Hemingway collectors to insure at least one chance for purchase. With the exception of the Guffey copies, each time since the war years that these copies have appeared they have brought higher prices—but only after the Guffey Sale have they brought record prices.

Hemingway's death in 1961 hardened the market on inscribed or association copies of both titles, particularly spectacular collector copies[9], with the felt assurance that comparable copies would not now appear to compromise market values.

What has happened to the charted prices of *iot* and *3 & 10*, has happened equally if not more dramatically to Hemingway autograph material. Here in the eyes of all scholars and librarians, as well as collectors, is real resource material.

In 1948 when the Sylvia Beach presentation copy of *3 & 10* appeared for the second time, someone had inserted an August, 1925, Hemingway autograph letter. The book brought less than it had the first time and less than a copy inscribed to Frank Hogan had brought just two years earlier. It is unlikely that the inserted letter influenced the price noticeably. Today, late signed typed letters of Hemingway with largely non-literary content easily command $500. So bullish is the market, that dealers buy wholesale at auction for stock. The twenty-five lots of Davis material that appeared at the Charles Hamilton Sale of May 24, 1967 brought $16,700—and were entirely bought in for dealer stock. Chances are virtually certain that the entire collection will turn over for equal or more than the 25% commission asked immediately following the sale.

For Hemingway at auction, the question remains—what prices will be realized at the next sale?[10]

APPENDIX

*Auction Record of Three Stories
and Ten Poems* [*3&10*] and *in our time* [*iot*]

1930

Selections From The Savage Library of Patterson, New Jersey. Ritter-Hopson Galleries. 10 March 1930. *iot* (99A), $160.00.

Puttick & Simpson. London. 7–8 May 1930. *iot* (458), £11/10.

1931

American Art Association - Anderson Galleries. 23 January 1931. *3&10* (109), $85.00.

Chicago Book & Art Auctions. 27–28 October 1931. *iot* (211), $88.00. *3&10* (212), $78.00.

Hodgson & Co. London. 25 November 1931. *iot* (204), £8/8.

1932

Scott Cunningham copy. Chicago Book & Art Auctions. 5–6 April 1932. *3&10* (179), $45.00.

Frank Irving Fletcher copies. American Art Association - Anderson Galleries. Part I. 19–21 April 1932. *3&10* (553), $130.00. *iot* (554), $140.00. Stamped "Review Copy." Inscribed "To Arthur Mers, from Ernest Hemingway. Paris, 1924."

1933

American Art Association - Anderson Galleries. 21 February 1933. *3&10* (117), $60.00. With TLS laid in. *iot* (118), $80.00. Presentation to Kate Buss.

American Art Association - Anderson Galleries. 6–7 December 1933. *iot* (318), $60.00.

1934

American Art Association - Anderson Galleries. 4–5 April 1934. *3&10* (338), $160.00.

Arthur M. Brown copy. Rains Auction Rooms. Key West, Florida. 19–20 April 1934. *3&10* (224), $22.50.

1935

American Art Association - Anderson Galleries. 24–25 April 1935. *3&10* (165), $110.00.

1936

American Art Association - Anderson Galleries. 29–30 January 1936. *3&10* (312), $230. Inscribed "For Sylvia from Hemingway August, 1923." *iot* (313), $190. Inscribed "To Sylvia Beach with love from Hemingway. March 1924"

Hodgson & Co. London. 4 March 1936. *3&10* (231), £7/15.

American Art Association - Anderson Galleries. 22–23 April 1936 *3&10* (252), $95.00. *iot* (253), $105.00.

American Art Association - Anderson Galleries. 9–10 December 1936. *3&10* (407), $130.00. Inscribed to Jo Davidson. *iot* (408), $65.00. Stamped "Review Copy." Inscribed "Compliments of the Author" (possibly in publisher's hand).

1937

American Art Association - Anderson Galleries. 13–14 January 1937. *iot* (273), $70.00.

American Art Association - Anderson Galleries. 14–15 April 1937. *3&10* (171), $60.00. *iot* (172), $47.00.

1939

Efrem Zimbalist copies. Parke-Bernet. 15–16 November 1939. *3&10* (178), $20.00. *iot* (179), $65.00.

1940

Burton Rascoe's copies. G. A. Baker. 16 January 1940. *3&10* (198), $42.00. Laid in, an autograph card from Hemingway to Rascoe. *iot* (199), $62.00.

G. A. Baker. 19–20 November 1940. *3&10* (199), $70.00. Inscribed. *iot* (200), $57.00.

1941

Parke-Bernet. 15–16 January 1941. *iot* (201), $55.00.

G. A. Baker. 15 April 1941. *iot* (138), $50.00. Inscribed to Kate Buss.

G. A. Baker. 7 October 1941. *iot* (136), $43.00.

H. Bertram Smith copies. Parke-Bernet. 10–11 December 1941. *3&10* (241), $65.00. *iot* (242), $50.00.

1944

Parke-Bernet. 18–19 April 1944. *iot* (493), $40.00.

1945

Frank J. Hogan copies. Parke-Bernet. Part I. 23–24 January 1945. *3&10* (239), $200.00. Inscribed "To Frank J. Hogan with all good wishes Ernest Hemingway." *iot* (240), $170,00. Inscribed "To Frank J. Hogan with two signatures Ernest Hemingway 1938 Ernest Hemingway (?)."

1947

Parke-Bernet. 13 January 1947. *3&10* (609), $90.00.

1948

Nathan N. Wallack copies. Parke-Bernet. 1 March 1948. *3&10* (189), $150.00. Inscribed to Sylvia Beach (P-B gives the year of the inscription as 1925 in the catalogue. In the catalogue for the 29-30 January 1936 sale, AAA has given the year as 1923. Presumably 1923 is correct.) With ALS laid in. *iot* (190), $150.00. Inscribed to Sylvia Beach.

1949

Frank Capra copies. Parke-Bernet. 26 April 1949. *3&10* (196), $120.00. Inscribed to James Richardson. *iot* (197), $160.00. Inscribed to James Richardson.

1951

E. W. Titus copies. Parke-Bernet. 8 October 1951. *3&10* (290), $120.00. *iot* (291), 130.00.

1952

Parke-Bernet. 29 January 1952. *iot* (273), $150.00.

1953

Parke-Bernet. 6 January 1953. *iot* (253), $80.00.

1954

City Book Auction. 1 December 1954. *3&10* (287), $120.00.

1958

Dr. Don Carlos Guffey copies. Parke-Bernet. 14–15 October 1958. *3&10* (151), $750.00. Inscribed "To Dr. Don Carlos Guffey with great admiration Ernest Hemingway." A second inscription "Dr. Don Carlos Guffey" on dust jacket (glassine sleeve ?). Laid in is a small card also inscribed to Guffey. *iot* (152), $900.00. Carries a 19 line inscription to Dr. Guffey concerning publication of *iot*.

Parke-Bernet. 10 December 1958. *3&10* (114), $350.00. *iot* (115), $475.00.

1959

Parke-Bernet. 28–29 April 1959. *3&10* (242), $400.00. Inscribed "To Dr. Don Carlos Guffey This book purchased at

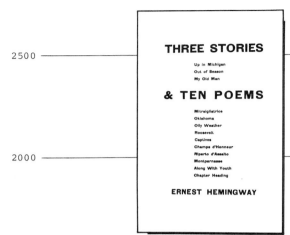

THREE STORIES

Up in Michigan
Out of Season
My Old Man

& TEN POEMS

Mitragliatrice
Oklahoma
Oily Weather
Roosevelt
Captives
Champs d'Honneur
Riparto d'Assalto
Montparnasse
Along With Youth
Chapter Heading

ERNEST HEMINGWAY

AUCTION RECORD

3000

2500

2000

1500

1000

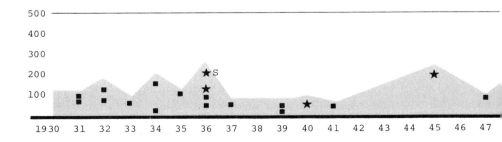

500
400
300
200
100

1930 31 32 33 34 35 36 37 38 39 40 41 42 43 44 45 46 47

★ — Signed, Presentation, or Association Copy

S — Copy inscribed to Sylvia Beach

R — Copy inscribed to James Richardson

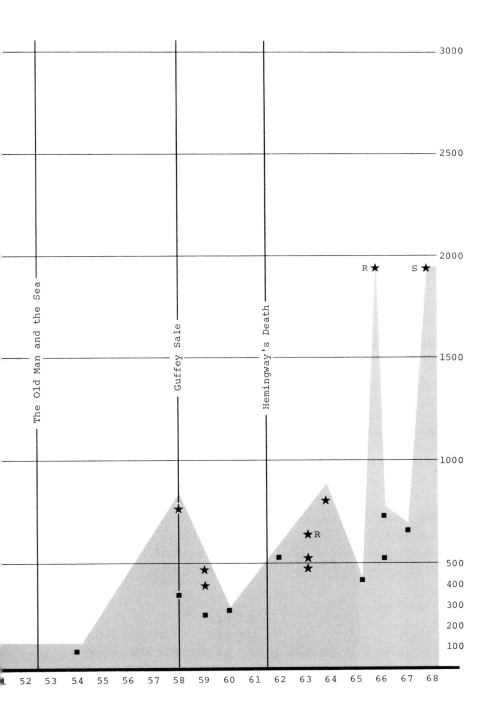

great expense by him hoping if he is to read he will not wait for the market to reach top. Ernest Hemingway." *iot* (243), $600.00. An 11 line inscription to Dr. Guffey concerning the frontispiece.

Whitman Bennet Sale. Parke-Bernet. 8 December 1959. *3&10* (425), $450.00. A 23 line inscription plus a 5 line insertion concerning McAlmon and The Contact Publishing Co. With an ALS and LS from Redman to Guffey. *iot* (426), $450.00. Inscribed "To Dr. Don Carlos Guffey With very best wishes. Ernest Hemingway."

1960

Parke-Bernet. 19-20 January 1960. *3&10* (262), $275.00.

1962

Jerome Kern copy. Parke-Bernet. 16 October 1962. *3&10* (137), $525.00. With ALS to Kate Buss.

1963

J. T. Chord copies. Parke-Bernet. 9 April 1963. *3&10* (188), $675.00. Inscribed "To James Richardson from Ernest Hemingway." *iot* (190), $725.00.

Parke-Bernet. 29 October 1963. *3&10* (148), $475.00. Signed.

1964

Parke-Bernet. 12 May 1964. *3&10* (82), $800.00. Signed. *iot* (83), $700.00. With the signature of Claude McKay.

1965

Parke-Bernet. 4 May 1965. *3&10* (155), $425.00.

1966

Parke-Bernet. 24 May 1966. *3&10* (89), $1900.00. Inscribed to James Richardson. *iot* (90), $900.00.

Max Weinberg copies. Swann. 6 October 1966. *3&10* (3), $700.00. *iot* (4), $925.00.

Swann. 13 October 1966. *iot* (195), $600.00.

Parke-Bernet. 2 November 1966. *3&10* (145), $525.00.

Sotheby. London. 6–7 December 1966. *iot* (389), £280.00.

1967

Sotheby. London. 12 July 1967. *3&10* (344), £270.

1968

Charles E. Feinberg copies. Parke-Bernet. Part II. 21–23 May 1968. *iot* (453), $2800.00. Inscribed to Sylvia Beach. August, 1923. *3&10* (457), $1900.00. Inscribed to Sylvia Beach.

---

[1] *Three Stories & Ten Poems.* Paris: Contact Publishing Co., 1923. Abbreviated as *3 & 10.*

[2] *in our time.* paris: three mountains press, 1924. Abbreviated as *iot.*

[3] Captain Cohn felt sufficiently bullish about this first Hemingway rarity to reach auction that he purchased it for his personal collection, exceeding his pre-sale limit by $10 in order to do so. The book was later inscribed for him by Hemingway and remains today in the magnificent Louis Henry Cohn Collection. The fact that it was a depression purchase is a further tribute to the buyer's conviction.

[4] Between 1930 and 1965, only one other copy of *iot* appeared at auction in England, and that was November 25, 1931, at Hodgson & Co., London. Price £8/8.

[5] A possibility exists that more than 170 copies of *iot* survived. Apparently a printing accident "spoiled" over a hundred copies of *iot* and the destiny of some remains in doubt.

[6] See Dr. Guffey's "Foreward."

[7] J. T. Chord Sale, Parke-Bernet, April 9–10, 1963; 48 lots brought $4842.50. Max Weinberg Collection, Swann Galleries, October 6, 1966; 170 lots brought $9442.50, Bill Davis material, Charles Hamilton, May 24, 1967; 25 lots brought $16,700.

[8] Charles E. Feinberg Sale, Parke-Bernet, Part II, May 21-23, 1968, lot 453.

[9] "Collector copies" in the sense sometimes used by librarians who apply the term to association or inscribed copies, a condition which they

feel lends insufficient bibliographical value to justify an exorbitant asking price—hence something only "collectors" would be foolish or extravagant enough to buy.

[10] The author gratefully acknowledges his debt to Miss Gloria A. Francis, Chief, Gifts and Rare Books Division, Detroit Public Library, to Mrs. Marguerite A. Cohn, House of Books, Ltd., and to Messrs. John S. Van E. Kohn and Bart Auerbach, all of whom have been generous with wise counsel and special knowledge.

"The Light of the World": Stan Ketchel as "My Sweet Christ"

By

Matthew J. Bruccoli

In his Preface to *The Fifth Column and the First Forty-nine Stories* (1938) Ernest Hemingway indicates that "The Light of the World" has been under-valued: "Reading them over, the ones I liked the best . . . and a story called 'The Light of the World' which nobody else ever liked."[1] As late as 1955 he was still concerned about "The Light of the World," according to A. E. Hotchner:

> Ernest cautioned me that the story was not as simple as it looked. He told me to think of it as a love letter to a whore named Alice who tipped the scales at 210. He said it was a story of illusion; that no one can really distinguish between how one was at a particular time in the past and how one is at the moment.[2]

Hemingway was right: the story is first-class Hemingway and merits more respect than it has received. The reason why it has been under-rated and generally misunderstood is that the meaning of the story depends on the irony of Stan Ketchel as a Christ figure; but few readers know enough about Ketchel (or Ketchell) to work out the meanings of the story.[3]

Stan Ketchel, "The Michigan Assassin," was the flamboyant middleweight champion between 1908 and 1910, when he was murdered. Born Stanislaus Kiecal (possibly Kaical or Klecal) in Grand Rapids, Michigan, in 1886 or 1887, Ketchel's first recorded professional fight was in 1903 at age sixteen or seventeen—by which time he had been a hobo and a bouncer in the mining camps of Montana. Between 1903 and 1910 he fought sixty-three bouts, winning forty-four by knock-outs. Ketchel won the title in 1908, lost it the same year to Billy Papke, and regained it the same year. His most famous bout came in 1909 when he fought Jack Johnson, the Negro heavyweight champion, in California amid considerable White Hope feeling. This fight became the source of legends and myths, some of them created by Ketchel's eccentric manager, Wilson Mizner. It is clear that Ketchel was heavily outweighed; his normal fighting weight was around 155, and Johnson was a 200-pounder. It has been alleged that the scales were rigged to reduce the official weight difference. *Nat Fleischer's The Ring Record Book and Boxing Encyclopedia* gives 170¼ vs. 205½.[4] Ketchel was knocked out in the twelfth after having floored Johnson in the same round. The generally accepted account is that there was an agreement between Ketchel and Johnson that they would put on an exhibition—even though the fight was billed as a title-bout—and that Ketchel tried to double-cross Johnson by knocking him out in the twelfth. Mizner claimed that the whole thing, including the two knock-downs in the twelfth, was fixed. Another version is that there was an agreement to coast the first ten rounds for the benefit of the movie cameras, after which the real fight would begin. Johnson—a notoriously unreliable man—reportedly told Dumb Dan Morgan, a boxing figure, that Ketchel did in fact knock him down. Since Johnson was also a notoriously vain man, his admission that Ketchel knocked him down is difficult to dismiss. All accounts, then, except Mizner's, agree that Ketchel—who was a savage puncher—actually did knock down Johnson, who outweighed him by thirty to fifty pounds and who is considered the greatest defensive boxer in the heavyweight division.[5] A high-liver and big-spender, Ketchel—who may have included opium among his dissipations—was burned out by 1910, when he was twenty-three or twenty-four, and went to a farm near Conway, Missouri, to recover his vigor. There he was shot by a farmhand named Walter Hurtz whom he rebuked for beating a horse. Goldie Smith, a servant on the farm, claimed that she was Hurtz's wife and that Hurtz was defending her honor; and it was generally accepted that the quarrel was over Goldie. Hurtz was really named Walter Dipley and was not married to Goldie under any name. They were tried as accomplices in a scheme to rob Ketchel and were both given long sentences.[6]

In addition to punching power and ring courage, Ketchel had a heroic appetite for women. He had a reputation for being extremely sentimental as well as having a passion for literature. Jim Tully, the hobo writer, is supposed to have called Ketchel the best-read man he ever knew—which takes in considerable territory, since Tully also knew H. L. Mencken.[7]

The title phrase "The Light of the World," occurs twice in the New Testament. In the Sermon on the Mount (Matthew 5:14) Christ addresses the believers as "the light of the world"; but the reference Hemingway probably had in mind is the episode of the woman taken in adultery (John 8:2–12): "I am the light of the world; he that followeth me shall not walk in darkness, but shall have the light of life." Carlos Baker suggests that the title is derived from Holman Hunt's painting, "I am the Light of the World." A copy of this painting was in a scrapbook Hemingway's mother made for him.[8]

In "The Light of the World" two whores claim Ketchel as their savior, the light of their world which at the time includes a hostile bartender, a homosexual, Indians, a nasty lumberjack, five whores, and the two boys of seventeen and nineteen who are passing through. That Ketchel was in no way a Christ figure is revealed by the facts of his life, but the problem is that he might have been a savior to the whores. Any reading of this story depends on which of four options the reader takes:

neither whore slept with Ketchel; both did; Peroxide did; Alice
did. My reading is based on the interpretation that Alice is telling the truth and that she was somehow enlightened by knowing
him.

Ketchel's name is first mentioned by the "shy man" who
says, "Cadillac is where Steve Ketchel came from and where
Ad Wolgast is from." This statement is half-right. Ad Wolgast—
lightweight champion from 1910 to 1912 and almost certainly
the model for Ad Francis in "The Battler"—was born in Cadillac; but Ketchel was born in Grand Rapids. The blonde whore
whom the narrator calls Peroxide immediately states that
Ketchel was shot by his father: "Yes, by Christ, his own father."
This is false, and so the connection between the deaths of Christ
and Ketchel is false; nevertheless nobody contradicts her, even
though the facts about Hurtz-Dipley were well known. The
only challenge to Peroxide's statement comes from the homosexual cook who asks if Ketchel's first name wasn't Stan, not
Steve. This is a difficult point: although Stanislaus Kiecal
fought as Stan Ketchel, he seems to have preferred being addressed as Steve. Instead of showing that neither whore knew
Ketchel, the Steve references could indicate that at least one of
them is pretending to a false intimacy with him. Peroxide continues to boast of her intimacy with Ketchel: "I loved him like
you love God . . . . Oh, my God, what a man he was I
hope to God they don't have fighters like that now. He was
like a god . . . . My soul belongs to Steve Ketchel." This is the
free-wheeling speech of a whore, but it is clear that Ketchel is
being deified. Along with these remarks she states that Johnson, "that black son of a bitch from hell," knocked out Ketchel
with a surprise punch when Ketchel turned to look at her—
which does not accord with any account of the fight. If anyone
threw a surprise punch, it was Ketchel. Peroxide's story is
weakest here, for she has to contradict herself and explain that
she went to the coast "just for that fight."

Alice, the 350-pound whore with the nice voice, then calls
Peroxide a liar, saying that Peroxide never knew Ketchel; but

that she did; and that he said to her, "You're a lovely piece, Alice." This is true, "to Jesus and Mary, true," says Alice crying. They match insults, with Alice getting the better of it as she says in her "sweet lovely voice" that Peroxide has had venereal disease whereas she is clean.

At this point the narrator is becoming interested in the logistics of sleeping with Alice, and his friend takes him out *to walk in darkness*—away from whatever light there is in the railway station.[9]

Although Alice fails to prove that she did know Ketchel, she is clearly more convincing than Peroxide. She avoids Peroxide's clichés and "stagey" speech—"my true, wonderful memories." Alice's emotion seems honest as she is moved to tears, and her voice is sincere. If we believe Alice—as I submit we must—then we have a story about a waste land partially redeemed, by a false savior. As Tom asks, "What the hell kind of place is this?" The distance between Stan Ketchel and Jesus Christ is absurd; nevertheless for Alice-in-waste-land who believed in Ketchel there is some light. Significantly, her first words in the story are, "Oh, my Christ . . . . Oh, my sweet Christ." For Peroxide there is no light, for she falsifies her belief in the Ketchel-savior.

The total meaning of "The Light of the World" depends on the narrator's response to this exposure to corruption and partial salvation. Although he is not named, the narrator here undergoes the same initiation as Nick Adams in "The Battler" (1924) or "The Killers" (1927). He encounters a form of evil and leaves, presumably to analyze the experience later. But "The Light of the World" departs from the Nick stories in that here the boy-young man is attracted to Alice who is both lost and saved through her faith in Ketchel. Nonetheless, her savior won't work for the narrator. "Tom saw me looking at her and he said, 'Come on. Let's go.' "

University of South Carolina

---

[1] Hemingway wanted to place "The Light of the World" first in *Winner Take Nothing* (1933), but was dissuaded by Maxwell Perkins. Hemingway

compared the story with one of his favorite works, Maupassant's "La Maison Tellier." Since these stories have little in common apart from whores, it must be assumed that Hemingway's comparison indicated his respect for the merits of "The Light of the World"—see Carlos Baker, *Hemingway The Writer as Artist* (Princeton: Princeton University Press, 1963), p. 140.

[2] Sleeve of *Ernest Hemingway Reading* (Caedmon TC 1185; 1965). One band on this record, "Saturday Night at the Whorehouse in Billings, Montana" gives Hemingway's experiences with the real 258-pound Alice; but since he also recounts his impossible experiences with Mata Hari, these recollections must be dismissed as a joke. It is to be noted that Alice's weight fluctuates in these reports.

[3] Baker sees the story as humorous. Philip Young in *Ernest Hemingway A Reconsideration* (University Park: Pennsylvania State University Press, 1966) correctly sees it as an initiation story. William Bysshe Stein ("Love and Lust in Hemingway's Short Stories," *Texas Studies in Literature and Language*, III [Summer 1961]) reads the story as presenting a travesty of Christian love which damns the narrator. The best readings are Joseph DeFalco's (*The Hero in Hemingway's Stories* [Pittsburgh: University of Pittsburgh Press, 1963]) and Sheridan Baker's (*Ernest Hemingway* [New York: Holt, Rinehart & Winston, 1967]) which see Ketchel as Christ-substitute. But no critic has conflated the facts of Ketchel's career with what is said about him in the story.

[4] New York: The Ring, 1953. My thanks to Mr. Fleischer for answering questions.

[5] Alvah Johnson, *The Legendary Mizners* (New York: Farrar, Straus & Young, 1952) discusses these theories about the Ketchel-Johnson fight and has considerable information about Ketchel.

[6] *New York Times*, 16 October 1910, 1.

[7] Alexander Johnston, *Ten—And Out!* (New York: Ives Washburn, 1947—3rd rev. ed.).

[8] *Ernest Hemingway A Life Story* (New York: Scribners, 1969), p. 606.

[9] There are interesting connections between "The Light of the World" and "A Clean, Well-Lighted Place." The stories were written at roughly the same time, and were coupled in *Winner Take Nothing* and *The Fifth Column and the First Forty-nine Stories*. In both, artificial illumination is contrasted with spiritual light, and it might be said that "The Light of the World" presents a dirty, partly-lighted place. See Daniel Barnes, "Ritual and Parody in 'A Clean, Well-Lighted Place' (*Cithara*, V [May 1966]) and Nicholas Cannady, Jr., "Is there any Light in Hemingway's 'The Light of the World'?" (*Studies in Short Fiction*, III [Fall 1965]).

Hemingway and the *New Masses*

By

John Unrue

In 1939 when one of the most crucial periods for determining
the course of modern American literature was coming to its end,
Lionel Trilling asserted that the critics of the radical Left had
exerted a damaging influence upon one of the most important
writers of twentieth century American fiction, Ernest Hemingway. Trilling was disappointed that Hemingway, "the man with
a dull personal ax to grind," had pushed aside "the artist" in his
two most recent books, *To Have and Have Not* and *The Fifth
Column and the First Forty-nine Stories.* And he especially ob-
jected to attempts "to settle the problem of the artist's relation
to politics by loudly making the requirement that he give up his
base individuality and rescue humanity and his own soul by becoming the mouthpiece of a party, a movement, or a philoso-
phy."[1] It is impossible to guage precisely the influence of the
radical Left upon a writer like Hemingway whose independence
is well known; however, that they as critics evaluated his work
from an obvious political bias and that they consistently sought
to convert him to their cause can be substantiated by reviewing
one organ of Marxian thought of the thirties, *New Masses.*

In 1932 when writers and critics, many of them major literary figures, commented in testimonial fashion in *New Masses*

about their conversions to the Left, Granville Hicks' remarks suggested the fervor and dedication that he felt for the Leftist movement. He discussed his function as a critic.

> I have no illusions, I trust the importance of criticism in this period of transition. The battle that is going on must be fought and won in quite a different arena. A person born in the middle class as I was, educated in bourgeois institutions, more or less professionally interested in literature, is poorly prepared to take a leading part. Yet the fight goes on on many fronts, and minor engagements as well as major must be fought and won. If the work for which I have been trained is not of primary importance, it is not without its own significance. Criticism must be a weapon if it is not to be merely an amusing game, and I know in what cause that weapon, so far as I am concerned, shall be wielded.[2]

For Granville Hicks Hemingway was not fulfilling the duty of a writer. He had not given up his isolation to seek truth in unity beside the other revolutionary writers.

The weapon that *New Masses* criticism had become was soon wielded. In *Death in the Afternoon* Hemingway had attacked Waldo Frank, one of the Left's leaders, and he was not to escape their wrath. Having learned that the December, 1934, issue of *Esquire* was to contain an article by Hemingway expressing annoyance at various Left-wing critics, Robert Forsythe severely attacked him. Forsythe declared that Hemingway was overly sensitive to criticism, and he chided him for not writing about the class struggle. Hemingway's excuse that one needed to be a member of the proletariat before he could write about the class struggle was unacceptable. After an attempt to demonstrate that Hemingway's "truth" was in fact relative, Forsythe continued, "Mr. Hemingway also possesses the queer notion that what a radical prefers is bad writing. We confess that we prefer a second-rate radical novel, with its *truth* and vitality and flame to the ordinary artistic production with its accumulation of preconceived and false ideas which are accepted as truth because it is safer to regard them in that way."[3]

Periodically the radical Left attempted to defend its position concerning the function of the writer against the propaganda label that had been given to much of the revolutionary literature of the thirties. In fact, Waldo Frank, himself, defended it. "There is no reason why good literature should not be of high documentary importance, and have strong political appeal. Indeed in a dynamic age like ours, a profound literary art, insofar as it must reveal the deepest evolving forces of man at the time, must be propaganda for these forces and the goal of these forces." Frank advised all revolutionary writers that oversimplified solutions to problems or "misplaced or forced direct-action" would result in, among other things, novels echoing "the bravado (hiding weakness) of the Hemingway-Dashiell Hamett school"[4]

The appearance of "Who Murdered the Vets?" in *New Masses* in September of 1935, however, won the admiration of the Left. Their hopes of winning Hemingway to their side increased considerably, and they used his dispatch as a cover article. It was introduced by an editorial denouncing the Roosevelt administration and wholly supporting Hemingway's view that the veterans had been cruelly abandoned. The editorial was even further dramatized by a drawing depicting the island piled with dead bodies and two overdressed politicians looking on.[5]

Nevertheless, even the salve of "Who Murdered the Vets?" was not strong enough to permit Granville Hicks to favorably review *Green Hills of Africa*. Apologetically, he confessed that he wanted to find something good to say because "Hemingway's piece in the *New Masses*, 'Who Murdered the Vets?' put me in a frame of mind to forgive anything, even *Death in the Afternoon*." Admittedly, *Death in the Afternoon* and *Green Hills of Africa* were "as good books as are likely to be written on bullfighting and hunting." However if Hemingway were to have succeeded by Hicks' standards, he would have had to find more suitable subjects. His advice to Hemingway was predictable, yet it is nonetheless astonishing.

Would Hemingway write better books if he wrote on different themes? "Who Murdered the Vets?" suggests that he would, for in that piece all his talents were suddenly lifted onto a higher level. This is why a great theme is important: It calls out so much more of what is in the author. I should like to have Hemingway write a novel about a strike, to use an obvious example, not because a strike is the only thing worth writing about, but because it would do something to Hemingway. If he would just let himself look squarely at the contemporary American scene, he would be bound to grow. I am not talking about his becoming a Communist, though that would be good for the revolutionary movement and better for him. I am merely suggesting that his concern with the margins of life is a dangerous business.[6]

Hemingway did not take Granville Hicks' advice about the strike novel.[7] The results would probably have been more disappointing than those of *The Fifth Column.* Therefore the Left was forced to continue waiting for Hemingway's proletarian novel. As late as 1934 *New Masses* was still clinging to *A Farewell to Arms.* They listed it in their advertisements and referred to it as an anti-war novel and one of "the great books that every worker and intellectual should own."[8]

On June 4, 1937, as Hemingway spoke to the Second Congress of American Writers in New York, the Leftists and Marxists undoubtedly thought that they were witnessing the true beginning of Hemingway's conversion. The editorial in *New Masses* on June 15, 1937, focused upon those views that were considered most compatible to the revolutionary movement. The Left wanted to emphasize that this important American writer would soon be counted as one of their own and that he was a new man. The congress, the editorial said, "reflects the increasing maturity of our men and women of letters in the face of those abrupt changes which mark contemporary society." It was noted also that the speakers, with the exception of Earl Browder, were "politically unattached." Nevertheless Archibald MacLeish, Donald Ogden Stewart, Murial Draper, Walter Duranty, and Ernest Hemingway "made it unmistakably clear that the fate of culture is inseparably bound up with the maintenance and extension of genuine democracy against the assults of Reaction." And to convince all that Hemingway was sympathetic with the movement, the editorial quoted from Hemingway's speech the line "there is only one form of government that cannot produce good writers, and that system is fascism."[9]

The text of Hemingway's speech was in fact not so completely political as *New Masses* would have it be; rather it again revealed Hemingway's great concern with the writer's responsibility to tell the truth and the difficulties that a war correspondent must encounter if he were to find that truth. The tone was one of passion as Hemingway indicated his disgust with the fascists' murdering of civilians, as he revealed his high regard for the Spanish people, and as he voiced his admiration for the international brigade; the tone was controlled, however, as he concluded his speech by pointing to the need for truth. It was indeed a speech with two points of view—the "man's" and the "artist's," and it exemplified effectively the very point that Hemingway was making. In the course of the speech when he heatedly discussed the fighting and the bravery, he was the "man." But when he talked about truth, he was the "artist," and he was true to his theory.[10]

Four months after the speech, *To Have and Have Not* appeared, and the Left was convinced that the long-awaited conversion of Ernest Hemingway was a reality. The novel was thought to have heralded not only Hemingway's new-found social conscience, but also, because of Hemingway's influence, perhaps a new direction in American literature. In his review of October 27, 1937, Granville Hicks fervently praised it. In Harry Morgan, Hemingway had come to realize an essential fact, "that no 'have not,' however brave, can single-handed defeat the 'haves.' " *To Have and Have Not* was better than *The Sun Also Rises* or *A Farewell to Arms.* "The explanation is quite simply," said Hicks, "his increasing awareness of the character of the economic system and the social order it dominates." Without this awareness, he continued, "his talents might easily have gone to waste."[11]

New Masses wasted no time; it used both *To Have and Have Not* and Hemingway to attract subscribers. The November 16, 1937 issue carried an advertisement announcing the new literary supplement that was to become a monthly feature beginning with the December 7 issue. A huge notice encouraged subscribers to fill in the provided blanks with ten names and to send them in with a dollar so that their friends might be reached by writers fighting for a better life. The advertisement was entitled: "ERNEST HEMINGWAY + Us + You = Santa Claus," and its explanation clearly indicated the significance that *New Masses* attached to the new novel.

> You don't get it? Let us explain. You've read Hemingway's new novel, *To Have and Have Not,* or you've read reviews of it. You know, as Granville Hicks said in his review of it in the *New Masses,* that it reveals in Hemingway "an increasing awareness of the character of the economic system and the social order it dominates." A very significant fact for American literature—a fact which reveals a whole new tendency in American letters, in which more and more leading writers are waking up to the historic necessity of joining in the fight for a better life.[12]

The following month another special Christmas offer was made to attract new subscribers. It was another appeal to subscribers to "Give a gift that counts!" at a time when "Even Santa Claus isn't safe." The gift was a package subscription plan enabling subscribers to order a six month or yearly gift subscription and a copy of twenty books that were favorably received by the Left. A year's subscription and a copy of *To Have and Have Not* could be purchased for $5.75.[13] *New Masses* also listed *To Have and Have Not* in its weekly recommended reading lists.

New Masses was determined to build an image for Hemingway to which even his Leftist critics would have been irresistibly drawn. On November 22, 1938, Edwin Berry Burgum wrote a long review in *New Masses* justifying nearly everything that Hemingway had written, even that which had been previously rejected by the Left. The preface to *The Fifth Column and the First Forty-nine Stories* was hailed as "one of the important literary documents of our time." The new Hemingway was depicted as a man who would turn his back on the past at the "risk of aesthetic failure" because of his awareness that "art must have its roots in social events." Hemingway had been tending toward this grand culmination for his entire lifetime, and he had at last reached the zenith of his literary career. "The whole of Hemingway's development," said Burgum, "from the beginning of his career as a writer is implicit in the character of Philip Rawlings. The collection of his short stories appended to the play graphs a course the direction of which the play can now be said to have defined."[14]

Burgum saw the course which Hemingway followed to get to *The Fifth Column* lined with fingerposts pointing to an inevitable triumph. If he "profited . . . from the more tolerant attitude that prevailed in literary circles as a result of the propaganda in the works of Mencken, Dreiser, and Anderson . . . he never stimulated criticism, as some of his predecessors had done, by justifying his interpretation." Admittedly, Hemingway had been candid about sex, and he did permit the "crude cynicism of popular speech to dominate his style"; however, "he did not conceal the redeeming sincerity of ordinary human impulse." Even *Death in the Afternoon* was now acceptable. Burgum said that the Left had forgotten "as events showed, that Hemingway had always lacked the principal ingredient of fascist culture." *Death in the Afternoon* was "one of those rare treatises by men of letters which discloses the gulf between scholarship and insight." The Spanish war was responsible for his final shift from Bohemianism to democracy and for his appreciation of the common man. *The Fifth Column and the First Forty-nine Stories*, asserted Burgum as he ended his essay, "is the record of the road that Hemingway has traveled through the confusions of modern life to a clearer insight into the relation between democracy and art."[15]

Obviously Burgum and other Leftist writers were delighted when Hemingway sent *New Masses* "On the American Dead in Spain," which appeared in the February 14, 1939, issue. It, too, was a lead story, and it was used to introduce an eight-page picture story on the Lincoln Battalion. In the "Between Ourselves" column, a weekly feature, were a picture of Hemingway and the comment that he sent with the article. " 'Here is the piece,' Hemingway wrote us from his home in Key West where he is at work between the wars. 'I've worked on it for five days . . . . this came down from three thousand words.' " And certainly it was a treasured "piece" to the editors. "We believe it is one of the finest tributes yet paid to the boys who won't be coming back."[16]

The Left thought that *To Have and Have Not* had been indeed a tribute to their influence, and soon the long-awaited book that Hemingway had been writing about the Spanish Civil War would be published. It was published, and they were stunned. Hemingway had betrayed them, and they suddenly decided that the man whose talents they had been extolling these past few years was in fact a man with considerably fewer talents than they had realized. Alva Bessie now summarized Hemingway's career in somewhat less flattering terms than did Edwin Berry Burgum. *To Have and Have Not* was not really the transitional book that it should have been. "Many expected that Hemingway's experience in Spain would so inflame his heart and his talents, that his long-announced novel of that war would be both his finest achievement and 'the' novel about Spain." Bessie lamented that "the individualism Hemingway's bourgeois critics so admired has led a man who is still one of our most greatly endowed creative artists" into a trap. Neither could he tolerate Hemingway's "cruel, vindictive, brutalized, irresponsible" portrayal of the Spanish people. It was also unacceptable that Hemingway praised the heroism of individual Communists and impugned and slandered their leadership. The final comment of Alva Bessie's review of *For Whom the Bell Tolls* is perhaps one of the most telling statements ever written by the Left in *New Masses*. "For at the moment he [Hemingway] is found in bad company; in the company of his enemies—clever enemies who will fawn upon him and use him, his great talents and his passion for the people's cause, to traduce and betray those talents and those people."[17]

Hemingway's attack on the Communist leaders in the Spanish Civil War was probably the most painful wound of all to the Left, and their spokesmen continued to denounce him as a betrayer of the people and a liar. Two weeks after Bessie's review appeared, Bernard Knox, who worked under Andre Marty, the Communist leader whom Hemingway portrays as a crazed killer in *For Whom the Bell Tolls,* wrote a six-column article in *New Masses* defending Marty. Marty was described in highly sentimental terms as a good and noble hero. Knox asserted that Hemingway had lied and that Marty was truly beloved by his men, none of whom was ever shot. His portrait of Andre Marty differs greatly from Hemingway's. Marty speaks to his troops, who have just finished a song praising him:

> As the song died away, the men who stood in the yard were no longer just so many men, they were a unit in an Army. And that was how Marty spoke to them. He spoke as no other man I have ever heard, so simply that in his mouth heroic words became bare statements of fact. Madrid was in danger, he told us. Soon it would be our duty and privilege to help defend it. We must use every minute left to prepare ourselves. We must do more than die, we must fight well, if fascism was to be destroyed. The silence as he finished was broken by shouts of "Vive Marty." And as he clenched his fist again in salute, the first company was already marching out the gate.[18]

The artist in Ernest Hemingway would not permit him to create such a version of Andre Marty; neither would it permit him to fall victim to an inflamed heart. Indeed, it was the artist's voice in the Writers' Congress speech which foretold the problems that *For Whom the Bell Tolls* would present. "It is very dangerous to write the truth in war and the truth is also very dangerous to come by."[19]

Ohio State University

---

[1] Lionel Trilling, "Hemingway and His Critics," *Partisan Review,* VI (Winter 1939), 52, 60.

[2] Granville Hicks, "Symposium," *New Masses,* VIII (September 1932), 5–10.

[3] Robert Forsythe, "In this Corner, Mr. Hemingway," *New Masses,* XIII (November 27, 1934), 26.

[4] Waldo Frank, "Values of the Revolutionary Writer," *New Masses,* XV (May 7, 1935), 19.

[5] *New Masses,* XVI (September 17, 1935), 1, 3, 9–10.

[6] Granville Hicks, "Small Game Hunting," *New Masses,* XVII (November 19, 1935), 23.

[7] It is indeed interesting that Richard Gordon, of *To Have and Have Not,* who is not an admirable character, should be unable to finish his novel about a strike in a textile factory.

[8] See *New Masses,* X (March 20, 1934), 31.

[9] "The Writers' Congress," *New Masses,* XXIII (June 15, 1937), 8.

[10] "Fascism is a Lie," *New Masses,* XXIII (June 22, 1937), 4.

[11] Review of *To Have and Have Not, New Masses,* XXV (October 26, 1937), 22–23.

[12] *New Masses,* XXV (November 16, 1937), 25.

[13] *New Masses,* XXV (December 14, 1937), 25.

[14] Edwin Berry Burgum, "Hemingway's Development," *New Masses,* XXIX (November 22, 1938), 21–23.

[15] *Ibid.*

[16] *New Masses,* XXX (February 14, 1939), 2. Certainly one would like to see what the editors deleted following "days" from Hemingway's Key West note.

[17] Alva Bessie, "Hemingway's *For Whom the Bell Tolls,*" *New Masses,* XXXVII (November 5, 1940), 25–29.

[18] Bernard Knox, "I Knew Andre Marty," *New Masses,* XXXVII (November 19, 1940), 15, 16.

[19] "Fascism is a Lie," 4.

2383 - mj

NOTE. This sketch has been prepared with a view to its inclusion in the next edition of WHO'S WHO IN AMERICA. If any important fact (conformatory to the plan of the book) has been omitted, it should be supplied. All blank spaces should be properly filled. Christian names should be given in full. Every sketch must receive approval of the editor to insure inclusion. Please revise and return immediately.

Return to THE A. N. MARQUIS COMPANY, 670 Cass Street, Chicago, Ill.

HEMINGWAY, Ernest, author; b. Oak Park, Ill., July 21, 1898; s. Clarence Edmonds and Grace (Hall) H.; ed. pub. schs. unmarried. Author: Three Stories and Ten Poems, 1923; In our Time, 1924; The Torrents of Spring, 1926; The Sun Also Rises, 1926; Men Without Women, 1927. Contbr. to Scribner's, Atlantic Monthly, New Republic, etc. Home: No Home 1 rue des Italiens, Paris, ###### France. Address: care Guaranty Trust Co. 140 Broadway, New York, N. Y. Charles Scribner's Sons, 5th ave and 48th Street New York, city N. Y.

JAN 13 1928

Leading essentials of every sketch are: Full Name, Place and Date of Birth, Full Names of Parents, Education, College Degrees (including dates) and Marriage (including full name and date).

Please furnish here both home and business address, if not correctly given above.
{ Home Address ...... Marie
{ Business Address .. Charles Scribner's Sons Fifth ave and 48th Street New York City

Returned [Date] ....19...... by ....
672-9   Printed in U.S.A.

141

Fitzgerald and Hemingway on Stage

By

Robert Emmet Long

The warring friendship of F. Scott Fitzgerald and Ernest Hemingway is the subject of a new play, *Before I Wake,* by Trevor Reese; the play opened October 13, 1968 at the Greenwich Mews theatre, located in the center of New York's Greenwich Village. There are only two characters in this Off-Broadway production—Fitzgerald, played by Martin Donegan, and Hemingway, played by Vincent McNally. The first of the two acts of *Before I Wake* is set in the 1920's, and begins with the first meeting of Fitzgerald and Hemingway; by the end of the act, their friendship has already cooled. Instead of expressing boyish admiration for the more famous Fitzgerald, as he does in the opening scene, Hemingway has begun to condescend. Act one closes with Hemingway's angry challenge to Fitzgerald: "Why, Scott, don't you realize that Zelda's crazy!"

The second half of *Before I Wake* dramatizes several meetings between the two novelists in the 1930's, with Fitzgerald languishing in the obscurity of a nearly forgotten novelist and Hemingway enjoying his role as an international celebrity. Yet they both live in their private hells—Fitzgerald's centering upon Zelda, and Hemingway's upon more obscure inner compulsions that are both creative and destructive. In the contrasting death scenes, with which the play concludes, Fitzgerald and Hemingway are still carrying on a rivals' duel with each other; their criticism of each other is qualified by a fundamental respect, and they sense that in some way their lives have been inseparably connected.

One of the central weaknesses of *Before I Wake* is exactly that the author has suggested a relation between the two writers which he cannot quite grasp; by the end it has eluded him. The play is merely a series of encounters, the dramatic significance of which is unclear. For this reason, *Before I Wake* fails to achieve a theme and a dramatic shape. While the newspaper critics unanimously condemned the play, they did not notice that the playwright had taken his dialogue (about ninety five per cent of it) from the letters of Fitzgerald and Hemingway—their letters to each other, and their letters to others commenting on each other. Playwrighting by quotation in this case proved very precarious, for the quotations seem stilted as conversation and appear to have strangled an imaginative creation of Fitzgerald and Hemingway. *Before I Wake* is merely a footnote to the sustained interest in the 1960's in the writing and careers of Fitzgerald and Hemingway. It suggests also, perhaps, that a scholarly study of the two, taken together, will at some time in the future be inevitable.

Queens College, CUNY

Books Received

Lloyd R. Arnold, *High on the Wild with Hemingway*. Caldwell, Idaho: Caxton, 1968. 343 pp. $9.95.

Carlos Baker, *Ernest Hemingway A Life Story*. New York: Scribners, 1969. 697 pp. $10.

Jackson J. Benson, *Hemingway. . .The Writer's Art of Self-Defense*. Minneapolis: University of Minnesota Press, 1969. 202 pp. $6.50.

Matthew J. Bruccoli, ed., *Fitzgerald Newsletter*. Washington, D.C.: Microcard Editions, 1969. $10.95.

Ernest Earnest, *Expatriates and Patriots American artists, scholars, and writers in Europe*. Durham, N.C.: Duke University Press, 1968. 310 pp. $10.

El Gran Gatsby. Havana: Editora Del Consejo Nacional De Cultura Editorial Nacional De Cuba, 1965. Includes "Retrato de Scott Fitzgerald," by Hemingway. Pirated.

Audre Hanneman, *Ernest Hemingway A Comprehensive Bibliography*. Princeton: Princeton University Press, 1967. 568 pp. $15.

Richard B. Hovey, *Hemingway: The Inward Terrain*. Seattle & London: University of Washington Press, 1968. 248 pp. $6.95.

John M. Howell, *Hemingway's African Stories: The Stories, Their Sources, Their Critics*. New York: Scribners, 1969. 169 pp. $2.75.

Katharine T. Jobes, ed., *Twentieth Century Interpretations of the Old Man and the Sea*. Englewood Cliffs, N.J.: Prentice-Hall, 1968. 120 pp. $1.25.

Nicholas Joost, *Ernest Hemingway and the Little Magazines: The Paris Years*. Barre, Mass.: Barre, 1968. 186 pp. $5.95.

Robert McAlman, *Being Geniuses Together*. Revised and with supplementary chapters by Kay Boyle. New York: Doubleday, 1968. 392 pp. $6.95.

Modern Fiction Studies, XIV (Autumn 1968). Ernest Hemingway Special Number.

Robert O. Stephens, *Hemingway's Nonfiction The Public Voice*. Chapel Hill: University of North Carolina Press, 1968. 391 pp. $8.50.

Fitzgerald Newsletter

Cover Illustration

The **Fitzgerald Newsletter**, nos. 1-40, is now available as a 327-page, hardbound book. The price is $10.95 ($9.95 if payment is enclosed).

Edited by
Matthew J. Bruccoli
University of South Carolina

Published by

NCR **MICROCARD® EDITIONS**
901 TWENTY-SIXTH STREET, N.W., WASHINGTON, D. C. 20037, 202/333-6393

INDUSTRIAL PRODUCTS DIVISION, THE NATIONAL CASH REGISTER COMPANY

F. Scott Fitzgerald

COLLECTOR'S HANDLIST

*This handlist
for
F. Scott Fitzgerald
collectors
describes
the first printings
of books
and
pamphlets
by Fitzgerald
and the
first book appearance
of material by him.*

Published by the
Fitzgerald Newsletter
the handlist
for bookcollectors
is
available
from
Matthew J. Bruccoli
31 Heathwood Cir.
Columbia, South
Carolina
for
$1.50